Majorca

COLLINS

Glasgow & London

First published 1990
Copyright © William Collins Sons & Company Limited
Published by William Collins Sons & Company Limited
Printed in Hong Kong
ISBN 0 00 435780-9

HOW TO USE THIS BOOK

Your Collins Traveller Guide will help you find your way around your chosen destination quickly and easily. It is colour-coded for easy reference:

The blue-coded 'topic' section answers the question 'I would like to see or do something; where do I go and what do I see when I get there?' A simple, clear layout provides an alphabetical list of activities and events, offers you a selection of each, tells you how to get there, what it will cost, when it is open and what to expect. Each topic in the list has its own simplified map, showing the position of each item and the nearest landmark or transport access, for instant orientation. Whether your interest is Architecture or Sport you can find all the information you need quickly and simply. Where major resorts within an area require in-depth treatment, they follow the main topics section in alphabetical order.

The red-coded section is a lively and informative gazetteer. In one alphabetical list you can find essential facts about the main places and cultural items - 'What is La Bastille?', 'Who was Michelangelo?' - as well as practical and invaluable travel information. It covers everything you need to know to help you enjoy yourself and get the most out of your time away, from Accommodation through Babysitters, Car Hire, Food, Health, Money, Newspapers, Taxis and Telephones to Zoos.

Cross-references: Type in small capitals - **CHURCHES** - tells you that more information on an item is available within the topic on churches. A-Z in bold - **A-Z** - tells you that more information is available on an item within the gazetteer. Simply look under the appropriate heading. A name in bold - **Holy Cathedral** - also tells you that more information on an item is available in the gazetteer under that particular heading.

Packed full of information and easy to use - you'll always know where you are with your Collins Traveller Guide!

Formentor

Castillian Spanish is the official language of Spain and Majorca. However the local dialect, Mallorquín, is widely used on the island to the extent that place names and signs appear in Mallorquín and/or Castillian with no overall consistency.

*Photographs by **Jan Kruse***

Pueblo Español, Palma

INTRODUCTION

The Balearic islands of Majorca, Menorca, Ibiza and Formentera, lie off mainland Spain's east coast and are the last outcrops in the Mediterranean of a mountain range which runs through southern Spain. They form the *Comunitat Autonoma de les Illes Balears*, one of Spain's 17 autonomous regions. Majorca, largest of the group, is roughly 100 km at its widest (E-W) and 75 km at its longest (N-S). It is delightfully varied geographically - high, rugged mountains, a rich agricultural plain and an indented coastline of 500 km along which lie pine-fringed beaches. Palma de Majorca, where over half the 600,000 Mallorquins live, is the historic but sophisticated regional capital.

In the summer peak, Palma airport is among Europe's busiest. It has about five million arrivals annually, mostly British and West German. Another half a million step off ferries from Barcelona, Valencia and elsewhere. Majorca is the single biggest destination in numbers for the European package holiday industry. What's the attraction? Undeniably the assurance of fine summer weather and good beaches. But as important, Majorca is where the holiday industry, Spanish and foreign, has invested more than elsewhere to provide lodging, food, entertainment and leisure facilities at hard-to-beat prices.

Holiday snobs dismiss Majorca as an island ruined by concrete jungles and mass tourism. They've got it wrong and it's their loss. No other Mediterranean island, and only a few other resort regions anywhere, presents such a variety of holiday choices. True, there has been development in a few parts but the tourist invasions don't leave many scars overall. Elitists who denigrate mass tourism are also decrying the wish of the majorityof their fellow citizens to enjoy affordable annual breaks with like-minded people in low-cost resorts. They also forget the economic health which large-scale tourism can bring to local people. It was Majorca's only cure and is its lifeblood.

For those who want inexpensive, brash, sometimes hard-edged and rowdy, almost home-from-home places under a hot sun, where fish and chips, *bratwurst* and *smorgasbrod* are always plentiful, resorts like Magaluff and Arenal are unbeatable. But most of the island's resorts are lower-key and quieter, and the development in some has been very gentle and sympathetic to the environment.

Sun, sea and sand, that's what most people are seeking and they are

seldom disappointed. Sports come first for others and the island caters
very well for them too, especially with watersports, sailing and tennis
facilities. Other opportunities for healthy excercise include walking or
riding through the picturesque countryside, strenuous hiking and
mountain climbing. Holiday complexes and businesses offer comprehensive sports and entertainment activities for all. Watersports and boat
trips are family favourites.

Out of the June to September high season Majorca attracts those whose
holiday priorities don't include big crowds and basking on a beach. In
spring the countryside is at its prettiest, autumn is like a good North
European summer. Winters are mild and the holiday industry caters
well for older people wanting long-stay breaks.

Long before the tourist boom started in the 1950s, Majorca had its
ardent aficionados and much of what charmed them still remains.
Pockets of rural life and inland villages are undisturbed, fishing com-
munities, though depleted, continue to land their catches, artistic people have saved threatened villages and decaying mansions and farm-
houses have been carefully converted into homes, hotels or restaurants.
The beautiful scenery and stunning seascapes remain untarnished.

The luxurious Hotel Formentor opened in 1929 and epitomizes the island's tradition of providing for upmarket holidays. More fine hotels, exclusive complexes, marinas packed with expensive yachts and an increasing number of golf clubs maintain a tradition which the local government wants to foster. The strongest evidence of Majorca's upmarket holiday element is the presence each summer of Spain's Royal Family at their holiday home on the island.

Sightseeing highlights are concentrated in Palma de Majorca, a compact city of narrow, evocative streets and noble buildings, which is dominated by its imposing Gothic cathedral. Sights around the island include limestone caves, isolated monasteries, medieval fortifications and the stone structures built by Majorca's prehistoric inhabitants. But in fact its attractive scenery, especially in the mountainous north west, makes the whole island a sightseeing attraction.

Palma has a good choice of smart shops and galleries, quality *artesanias* and interesting markets. Some resorts have modern fashion boutiques and arts and crafts shops. Every village has its weekday market. Craftsmen can be seen making items for sales. Blown glass, artificial pearls and leathergoods can be good buys.

Cultural life is centred on Palma's museums, art centres, exhibition halls and its venues for music, dance and drama. Towns like Denia, a haven for creative foreigners, compete on a smaller scale. Other places have music festivals and exhibitions of works by local and foreign artists. What remains of popular music and dance traditions is best seen at village fiestas or family celebrations.

Big tourist hotels and many restaurants play safe with bland international menus but traditional island cooking presents simple, tasty dishes of local fish, meat (mostly pork) and vegetables in hearty portions at good prices. For fine dining, not only in the pricier places, there's the Majorcan version of the lighter, new-style Mediterranean cooking.

Nightlife in the resorts centres on their discos, some rather tatty, others modern and with all the laser gear. In Magalluf, there's the extraordinary BCM, as well as a casino and big night club. Palma's El Terreno district has the best variety. Barbeques with shows of Spanish dancing or medieval tournaments are other options. But on Majorca's balmy nights there's a strong temptation to do no more than sit on a terrace, or by the beach, sipping the local wine.

ellencs

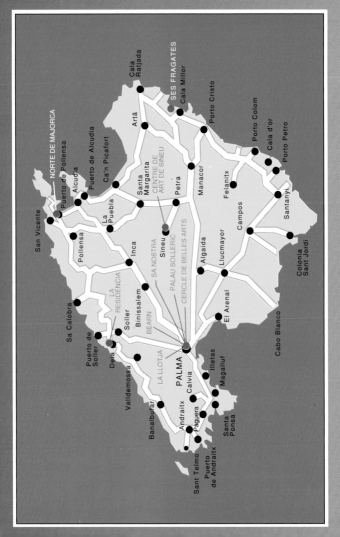

CERCLE DE BELLES ARTS Unió 3, Palma.
• 1100-1330,1800-2100 Mon.-Sat.
Changing exhibitions in the Casa Balaguer, home of the fine arts circle.

LA LLOTJA Paseo Sagrera, Palma.
• 1000-1300,1700-2100 Mon.-Sat., 1000-1330 Sun. and hols.
Modern art in splendid Gothic surroundings. See **BUILDINGS - PALMA**.

PALAU SOLLERIC San Cayetano 10, Palma.
• 1100-1330,1700-2030 Tues.-Fri., 1100-1330 Sat.
There are regular shows of contemporary art in this handsome palace.

SA NOSTRA Ramón Llull 2, Palma.
• Business hours.
Salon of the Caixa de Baleares (savings bank) has changing exhibitions.

BEARN Concepción 6, Palma.
• Business hours.
Palma has a good selection of commercial galleries featuring the work of local and foreign artists. This is one of a number along this street.

LA RESIDENCIA On main road north of Deia.
• Variable.
Smart hotel holding regular exhibitions. There are more galleries in the village, which is home to many artists.

NORTE DE MALLORCA
Paseo Anglada Camarasa 85, Puerto de Pollensa.
Features local artists. More galleries in port area and Pollensa town.

SES FRAGATES Av Ingeniero Antonio Garau, Cala Bona.
One of several new contemporary art galleries in the east coast resorts.

CENTRE DE ART DE SINEU
Changing exhibitions, mostly of Majorcan artists. A reminder to look out for something similar in other inland towns.

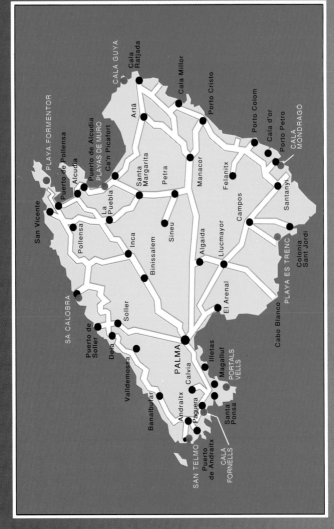

PORTALS VELLS
Boat excursion from Palma (Paseo Marítimo - Auditorium), Magalluf (Hotel Trinidad) and Cala D'Or.
Easy access from Magalluf. To the south, less developed, is Cala Figuera. Through pine woods to tiny Playa Mago, the island's official nudist beach.

CALA FORNELLS
Peaceful beach near the resorts of Santa Ponsa, Paguera and Camp de Mar.

SAN TELMO
Boat excursions form Palma, Paguera (Hotel Mar i Pins), Puerto Andraitx and Puerto Soller.
Facing Dragonera island, pretty cove with fine sand and rocks.

SA CALOBRA
Boat excursion from Puerto Soller. Access via a switchback road.
You can either swim in the sea or the freshwater of the Torrente de Pareis.

PLAYA ES TRENC
Part of stretch of fine sand from Colònia de Sant Jordi to La Ràpita.
Pines, dunes and good amenities. Some unofficial nudism.

PLAYA FORMENTOR
Boat excursion from Puerto Pollensa and Puerto Alcudia.
Pine-backed beach of silken sand.

PLAYAS DE MURO
Pine-shaded, thin ribbon of fine sand and very gently sloping beach.

CALA GUYA
Good amenities, some sand dunes and a protected stretch of beach.
More isolated Cala Mezquida is a short hike to the north.

CALA MONDRAGÓ
Convenient to Cala D'Or and Porto Petro, relatively undeveloped cove with good beach-fun amenities.

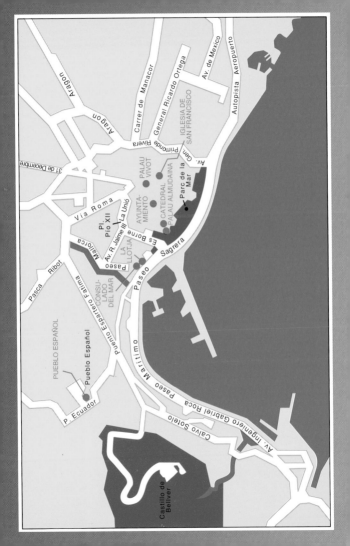

Palma

CATEDRAL Pl Almoina.
•1000-1230, 1600-1830 Mon.-Fri. 1000-1400 Sat. Closed holidays.
La Seo is one of the largest cathedrals designed in the Gothic style. It took 370 years to complete from its conception in 1230.

PALAU ALMUDAINA Pl Almoina.
Guided tours. •0945-1300, 1615-1800 Tues.-Fri. 0945-1300 Sat.
Closed holidays.
Built by the Moors, then a palace of Majorca's kings, it was restored in the 1960s. Classed as a royal palace and used for state functions. See MUSEUMS.

IGLESIA DE SAN FRANCISCO Pl San Francisco.
•0930-1300, 1530-1900 Mon.-Sat., 0930-1300 Sun. and hols.
Gothic church with Baroque facade and attractive cloister.

LA LLOTJA Paseo Sagrera.
See ART GALLERIES.
15thC commercial exchange designed with military features. Outstanding example of Gothic civil architecture.

CONSULADO DEL MAR Paseo Sagrera.
•Not open to public.
Renaissance building (17thC). Originally a trade and shipping exchange, now offices of the Gobern Balear (Balearics Regional Government).

PUEBLO ESPAÑOL Capitán Mesquida Veny.
•0900-2000. Craft workshops 1000-1800 (closed Sunday).
Showpiece village with replicas of famous Spanish buildings.

AYUNTAMIENTO Pl de Cort.
The Town Hall has a notable Baroque facade from the 17thC.

PALAU VIVOT Zavella 2.
•Variable. Also by written application.
Noble family's mansion. Attractive patio and elegant staircase. Some interesting tapestries and furniture.

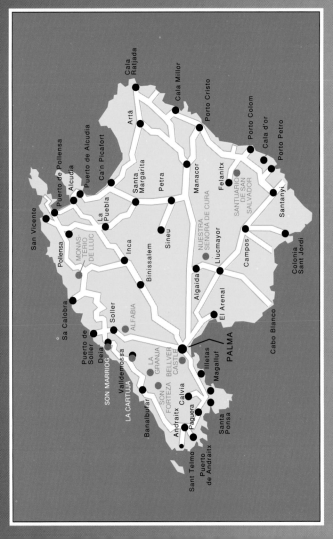

Island

MONASTERIO DE LLUC Escorça.
•1000-1900 -Summer, •1000-1730 Winter.
The island's principal monastery in a barren mountain setting. Pilgrims venerate the bejewelled statue of the Virgin of Lluc. A boys' choir sings at noon.

NUESTRA SEÑORA DE CURA Ctra Algaida - Llucmayor.
Small monastery on Mount Randa with wide views across the central plain.

SANTUARIO DE SAN SALVADOR Crta Felanitx-Porto Colom.
Picturebook monastery from the 14thC. Panoramic views.

SON MARRIOG Deia.
•0930-1430, 1630-2000 Mon.-Sat. 0930-1430 Sun. (Summer).
Large, clifftop mansion of Archduke Ludwig Salvator with its collection of furniture, paintings, ceramics and books. Beautiful views from the mirador.

LA CARTUJA Valldemossa.
•0930-1330, 1500-1830 Mon.-Sat. (1730 in winter).
Monks left this monastery in the 1830s. A few rooms contain items associated with Chopin and George Sand's brief stay in 1838.

LA GRANJA Esporlas.
•1000-1900 Summer. •0930-1700 Winter.
*Large manor house of the Fortuny family. See **CRAFTS & CUSTOMS**.*

ALFABIA Crta Bunyola-Soller.
•0930-1830 Mon.-Sat. (Summer), 0930-1700 Mon.-Sat. (Winter).
*Jaime I (see **A-Z**) gave this estate to an Arab who helped him conquer the island. Moorish influence is evident in the luxuriant gardens.*

SON FORTEZA Puigpunyent.
Fine example of the many country houses of important island families.

BELLVER CASTLE above El Terreno.
•0900 to sunset.
Built in the 14thC. Grand panoramas from the battlements.

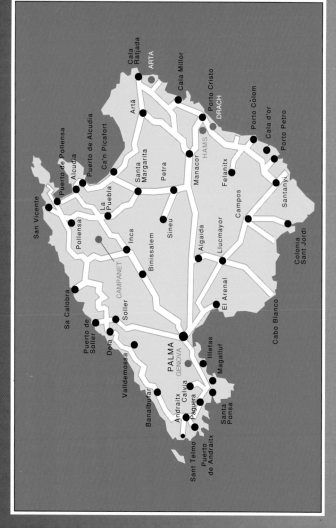

DRACH Porto Cristo.
Guided tours with concert.
• 1000 - 1700, (on the hour) Summer.
• 1100, 1200, 1400, 1500 (and, without concert, 1600, 1700) Winter.
Drach means dragon in Catalan. Crowds flock to join the guided tours of Majorca's best-known caves. Stalagmites and stalactites with imaginative names are beautifully lit. A sound-and-light concert across the long and deep Lago Martell provides a memorable finale. No photography permitted.

ARTA Playa de Canyamel.
9 km SE of Arta.
• 0930-1900 Summer, 0930-1700 Winter.
Said to have inspired Jules Verne's Journey to the Centre of the Earth. Limestone headland eroded by water with caverns 300 m deep and 45 m high. Entrance through a huge slit in the cliff and some steep walking inside.

HAMS Porto Cristo.
Guided tours with concert, every 15 min.
• 1030-1320, 1445-1630 (and to 1730 without concert) Summer,
• 1100-1320, 1415-1530 Winter.
Named after the fishhook formations in the Sueño de un Angel ('angel's dream') cavern. Smaller than the nearby Cuevas del Drach, but no less fascinating in the variety of formations, caverns and illuminations. A brief lakeside concert is included. Socavón show with flamenco, regional and classical dancing is held at 2130 on Sundays.

CAMPANET Near Campanet, off Ctra Palma-Alcudia.
• 1000-1930 Summer.
• 1000-1800 Winter.
Fewer tourists visit these small caves although they have well-illuminated rock formations.

GENOVA Genova.
• 0900-2400.
Tiny by comparison with the others but very conveniently located near Palma and the Palma Bay resorts.

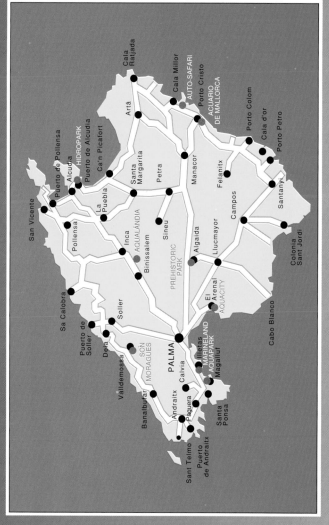

AQUACITY El Arenal, at end of motorway.
•1000-2000. Bus every 20min.
One of the largest water fun-fairs in the world.

AQUAPARK Ctra Cala Figuera-Magalluf.
•1000-2000. 15 Apr.-31 Oct.
Long-established and well-maintained. All the usual waterslides and thrills.

AQUALANDIA Ctra Palma-Inca, N of Binissalem.
•0900-2000.
Water toboggan, swimming pool, mini-golf, craft and souvenir shops.

HIDROPARK Av Tucán, Puerto Alcudia.
•1000-2000.
One of the few attractions for very young holidaymakers in the area.

MARINELAND Costa d'en Blanes.
•Shows 1030-1230,1500-1700. Closed 20 Nov.-25 Dec.
Performing dolphins and sea lions. Highly recommended.

ACUARIO DE MALLORCA Next to Cuevas Drach, Porto Cristo.
•0900-1900.
Small aquarium with exotic fish from all around the world.

AUTO-SAFARI Ctra Porto Cristo-San Servera.
•Summer 0900-1900. Winter 1900-1700.
A 4 km drive (own car or group) through meadowland where elephant, rhino, giraffe, zebras, antelope, deer and monkeys roam.

SON MORAGUES Valldemossa.
•1200. Closed Sat. & Sun. in winter.
Family fun with donkey rides along country paths.

PREHISTORIC PARK Ctra Palma-Manacor.
•1000-2000.
30 life-size models to see in a pinewood park with lake and waterfalls.

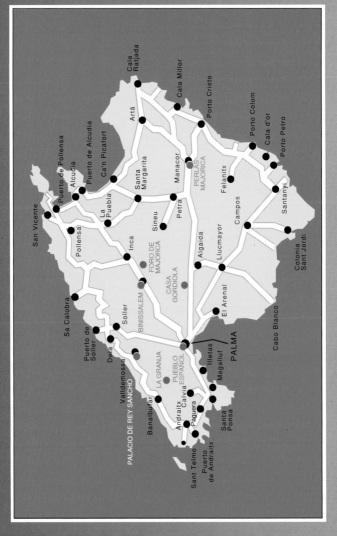

PUEBLO ESPAÑOL
Capitán Mesquida Veny, Palma.
•1000-1800 Mon.-Sat.
Craftsmen make and sell ceramics, glassware, leathergoods, enamelwork, gold and silver jewellery. See BUILDINGS, **Palma**.

LA GRANJA
Esporlas.
•1530-1700 Wed. and Fri.
Weaving, embroidery, pottery and carpentry done the old way. Displays of regional dancing in traditional costumes. See BUILDINGS, **Island**.

CASA GORDIOLA
Ctra Palma-Manacor, W of Algaida.
•0900-1300, 1500-2000 (1900 in winter) Mon.-Sat., 09-00-1200 Sun.
Glassblowing by skilled artisans. Shop and small museum.

PERLAS MAJORICA
Via Roma, Manacor.
•0900-1230, 1500-1900 Mon.-Fri., 1000-1300 Sat. & Sun.
Tour of factory making artificial pearls. Tempting shop.

FORO DE MALLORCA
Ctra Palma-Inca, N of Binissalem.
•1545 Tues & Fri.
Island music and dancing by Agrupació Aires de Muntanya. See CHILDREN.

BINISSALEM
Pl de la Iglesia, Binissalem.
•1030 & 1130 Fri.
Folk-dancing in the church square.

PALACIO DE REY SANCHO
Valldemossa.
•1100 Mon. & Thurs.
Folk music and dance. See BUILDINGS, **Island**.

Boat

This list of departure points and destinations gives an idea of the many trips available. Check locally about timings, prices and other trips.

PALMA
Magalluf. Portals Vells. Puerto Andraitx and San Telmo. Colònia Sant Jordi. Cabrera.

PALMA NOVA/MAGALLUF
Cala Vinyes, Cala Figuera and Portals Vells. Marineland. Palma Fleamarket.

PAGUERA
Palma. Marineland. Santa Ponsa & Islas Malgrats. San Telmo and Dragonera.

PUERTO ANDRATX
San Telmo and Dragonera.

PUERTO SOLLER
La Calobra and Torrente de Pareis. Cala Deia. Sa Forada. La Dragonera. Cala San Vicente.

CA'N PICAFORT
Cap Farrutx. Cap de Menorca. Cap de Formentor. Trips to Playa Formentor from Puerto Pollensa and Puerto Alcudia.

CALA RATJADA
Canyamel (Cuevas de Arta).

CALA MILLOR
Cala Ratjada. Porto Cristo.

CALA D'OR
Palma Nova, Magalluf and Portals Vells.

Coach & Train

WEST COAST
*Camp de Mar. Puerto Andraitx. Estellenchs. Coll d'es Pi. Banyalbufar.
Esporlas. La Granja (see* BUILDINGS 2, CRAFTS & CUSTOMS*).*

CUEVAS DE DRACH
Casa Gordiola and Perlas Majorica (see CRAFTS & CUSTOMS*). Porto Cristo.
Acuario de Mallorca (see* CHILDREN*). Cuevas de Drach (see* CAVES*). Auto-
Safari (see* CHILDREN*).*

SANTUARIO DE SAN SALVADOR
Felanitx. Santuario de San Salvador (see BUILDINGS 2*). Porto Colom.
Cala D'Or. Ses Salines. Cap o Corp Vell (prehistoric site). Cabo Blanco.*

LLUC AND CALOBRA
Inca. Selva. Monasterio de Lluc (see BUILDINGS 2*). Torrente de Pareis.*

FORMENTOR
Playa Formentor (see BEACHES*). Inca. Foro de Mallorca (see* CRAFTS & CUS-
TOMS*). Museo de Cera (wax museum).*

VALLDEMOSSA
Cartuja. Valldemossa. Son Marroig (see BUILDINGS 2*). Puerto Soller.
Jardines de Alfabia (Moorish gardens).*

ALCUDIA
Sineu. Petra (birthplace of Junipero Serra, see A-Z*). Playas Ca'n Picafort.
Puerto Alcudia.*

CUEVAS ARTA
Prehistoric Park (see CHILDREN*). Perlas Majorica (see* CRAFTS & CUSTOMS*).
Cuevas de Arta (see* CAVES*). Playa de Canyamel. Auto-Safari (see* CHILDREN*).*

SOLLER & PUERTO SOLLER
Train departs 0800,1040, 1300, 1515, 1945; returns 0645, 0915, 1150,
1410, 1820 (and 2100 Sun. only). From station at Palma's Pl España.
Enjoy the varied scenery as the quaint train rattles along the narrow track.

Santuario de San Salvador

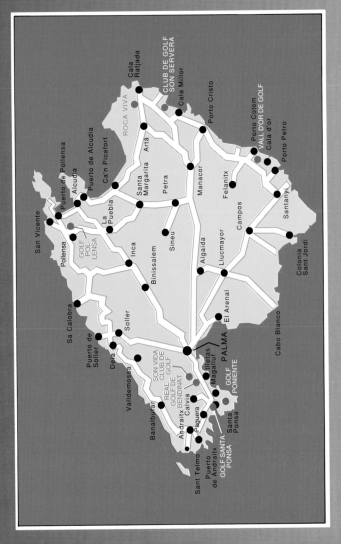

GOLF SANTA PONSA Urbanización Santa Ponsa, 07184 Calvia. Telephone 69 02 11.
18 holes. Venue of the first Mallorca Open de Baleares in 1988 and currently regarded as the island's top course.

SON VIDA CLUB DE GOLF Urbanización Son Vida, 07012 Palma de Mallorca. Telephone 23 76 20.
18 holes. Generally long and flat with big greens. Island's oldest course in well established, exclusive hotel and residential area.

GOLF PONIENTE Ctra Cala Figuera, Calvia. Telephone 68 01 48.
18 holes. Long and difficult with large, fast greens.

REAL GOLF DE BENDINAT Urbanización Bendinat, 07184 Calvia.Telephone 40 52 00.
9 holes. Elevated tees, sloping fairways and quite difficult greens.

GOLF POLLENSA Ctra Palma-Pollensa, 07460 Pollensa. Telephone 53 32 16.
9 holes. Friendly to high handicaps. Good facilities include tennis courts and children's nursery.

CLUB DE GOLF SON SERVERA Urbanización Costa de los Pinos, 07550 Son Servera.
Telephone 56 78 02.
9 holes. Few gradients, narrow fairways and fast greens.

VALL D'OR CLUB DE GOLF Ctra Porto Colom-Cala D'Or. Postal - Apartado 23, 07660 Cala D'Or.
Telephone 57 60 99.
9 holes. Open and fairly flat holes among olive, carob and palm trees.

ROCA VIVA Camp Mitjà, Apartado 6, Capdepera. Telephone 56 34 04.
18 holes. Under construction at time of going to print..

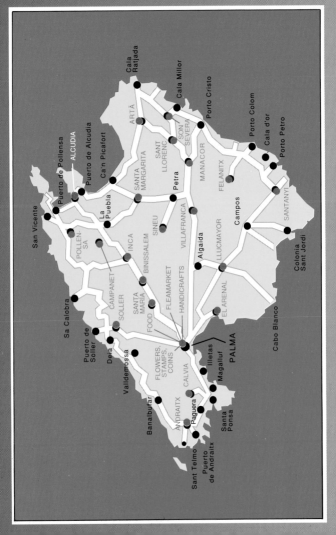

FLEAMARKET
c/Honderos, Polígono de Levante.
0800-1400 Sat. Bus 5-15.
Lively El Rastrillo is the island's biggest market for household goods, junk, trinkets and, perhaps, a rare bargain.

FOOD
Weekday mornings.
Covered market in Pl Olivar has tempting displays of fruit, vegetables and fish. Also Santa Catalina market in Pl Navegación and Mercat del Tenis, c/ Juan Crespi.

HANDICRAFTS
Pl Mayor. Fri. & Sat. mornings.
Professionals and amateurs have a chance to show and sell their crafts.

FLOWERS, STAMPS, COINS
La Rambla (Via Roma).
Colourful stalls along this tree-lined paseo.

INCA
Pl Mayor and adjoining streets, Inca.Thurs morning.
Big, all-sorts market sustained by tourists. Lots of leather items.

SINEU
Pl del Mercado, Sineu.
Wed. Early morning.
Genuine atmosphere of a traditional agricultural fair with livestock sales.

OTHER TOWNS
Travelling stallholders and townspeople offer housewares, clothes and trinkets on regular market days in the following towns: Mon.: Calvia, Manacor. Tues.: Alcudia, Campanet, Santa Margarita. Wed.: Andratx, Santanyi, Villafranca. Thurs.: Arenal, Sant Llorenc. Fri.: Llucmayor, Son Servera. Sat.: Santanyi, Soller. Sun.: Arta, Binissalem, Felanitx, Pollensa, Santa Maria.

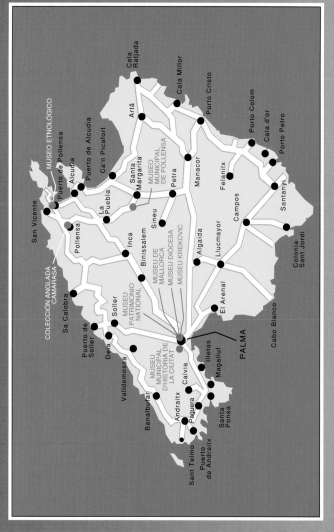

MUSEU DE MALLORCA Portella 5, Palma.
• 1000-1400, 1600-1900 Tues.-Sat., 1000-1400 Sun.
Archaeological items, medieval paintings, altar pieces and ceramics.

MUSEO PATRIMONIO NACIONAL
Palau Almudaina, Pl Almoina, Palma.
• Guided tours 0945-1300, 1615-1800 Tues.-Fri., 0945-1300 Sat.
*Furnishings, paintings, tapestries and armour. See **BUILDINGS -PALMA**.*

MUSEU DIOCESA Mirador 7, Palma.
• 1000-1300, 1500-1800 Mon.-Sat., 1000-1300 Sun.
In the Episcopal Palace. Archaeology, interesting ceramics and glassware, medieval paintings and religious sculptures.

MUSEU MUNICIPAL D'HISTÒRIA DE LA CIUTAT
Castell de Bellver. • 0900 to sunset Mon.-Sat.
A few prehistoric pieces and coins of specialist interest.

MUSEU KREKOVIC Ciudad de Queretaro, Poligono de Levante.
• 1030-1330 Mon.-Sat.
Works by the Yugoslav painter. Vivid paintings depicting Inca and Peruvian themes. A Hispano-American cultural centre.

MUSEO ETNOLÓGICO C/ Mayor, Muro.
• 1000-1400, 1600-1900 Tues.-Sat., 1000-1400 Sun.
Farming and craft tools, traditional clothes, ceramics in a 17thC building.

COLECCIÓN ANGLADA CAMARASA Paseo Anglada
Camarassa 87, Puerto Pollensa. • Closed 1600-1930 Wed. & Sun.
*Studio home of the Catalan/French artist (see **A-Z**). Monographs, paintings, costumes and fans.*

MUSEO MUNICIPAL DE POLLENSA Convento de Santo
Domingo, Pollensa. • 1000-1200 Tues., Thurs., & Sun.
A Baroque altar piece, medieval art and the winning entries from the annual art competitions.

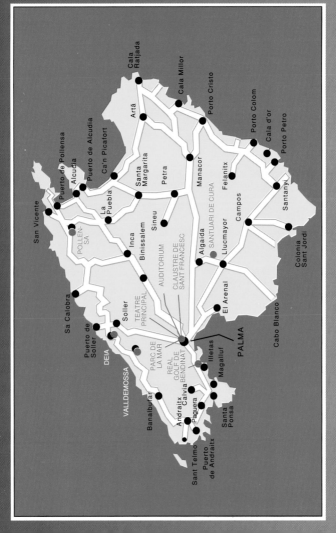

MUSIC ▪ DANCE ▪ DRAMA

TEATRE PRINCIPAL Pl Weyler.
•Performances usually start at 2200.
Varied programme of local and visiting theatre and dance groups.

AUDITORIUM Paseo Marítimo 18.
•Performances usually start at 2200.
Bigger venue for concerts, opera, ballet and theatre.

PARC DE LA MAR
•Mostly around 1200.
Open-air venue for music and dance groups.

CLAUSTRE DE SANT FRANCESC Pl Sant Francesc (San Francisco).
Annual Serenates d'Estiu classical concerts in lovely cloister.

POLLENSA Claustre de Sant Domingo.
•July-September.
The Festival de Pollensa continues to attract international soloists and orchestras.

DEIA Son Marroig, Parc Municipal, Esglesia.
•June-September Festival Internacional de Deia.
Well-known and less familiar music and performers in delightful settings.

REAL GOLF DE BENDINAT Urb Bendinat, Calvia.
•July-September.
Concerts a l'Herba. Island soloists, choirs and chamber orchestras.

SANTUARI DE CURA Puig Randa, off Ctra Algaida-Llucmayor.
•July-August.
Just a few concerts in a superb location.

VALLDEMOSSA Claustre Cartoixa (Cartuja).
•August. Festivals Chopin.
International musicians play works of Chopin and others.

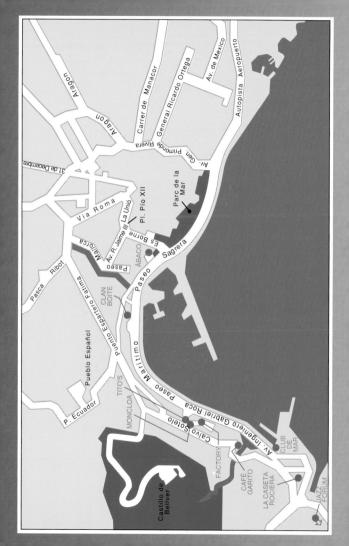

Palma

Central Palma is quiet at night. Apuntadores is the liveliest street and there's some activity in Es Jonquet. Most of the action is in El Terreno. Many places are closed on Sunday.

CAFE GARITO Darsena de Ca'n Barbara.
Relaxed ambience. Interesting art shows. And Rafa mixes good cocktails.

CLUB DE MAR Paseo Marítimo (Club de Mar).
High-priced drinks in this music bar/disco. Favourite of international 'yachties' and Palma's wealthy class. Selective about clientele.

FACTORY Pl Mediterráneo.
Palma's very young set gather until 0700 in this music bar which looks like an early 1900s factory.

TITO'S Entrance off Pl Gomila and Paseo Maritimo.
Palma's top disco. Big place with good sound and light systems. Grand views of bay. Live performances.

MONCLOA Pl Gomila, El Terreno.
Spanish and international music in this late night rendevous of the PoMo set. Terrazas overlook the plaza.

CLAN BOITE Pl Vapor (Es Jonquet).
Listen and dance to good music in this elegant and luxurious disco bar.

ÁBACO San Juan 1.
Go before or after dinner for exotic, expensive cocktails among huge displays of fruit and vegetables in this renovated palace.

LA CASETA ROCIERA Paseo Marítimo (Porto Pi).
This is a good place to see flamenco artistes and join the craze for dancing sevillanas.

JAZZ FORUM Av Joan Miró 292 (Cala Mayor).
Island's best venue for enjoying jazz. Go around midnight.

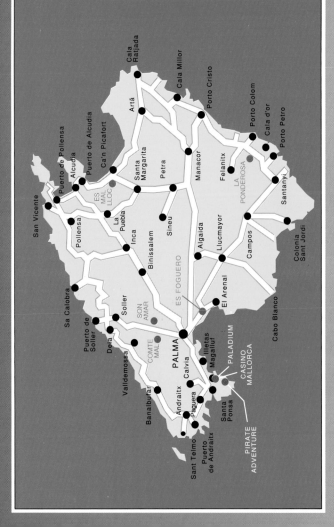

Dinner & Show

Most of the places listed below are destinations for organised excursions.

ES FOGUERO Ctra Palma-Santanyi (end of motorway).
• Dinner 2030. Show 2230. Mon.-Sat. (Summer), Wed.-Sat. (Winter).
Spanish dancing - traditional and contemporary. Followed by cabaret acts.

CASINO MALLORCA Urb. Sol de Mallorca, Magalluf.
• Gaming rooms 1700-0400, restaurant 1030-0100.
Roulette, Blackjack, Craps, etc. Slot machines. Passport essential.

PALADIUM Casino Mallorca.
• Dinner 2000, show 2200 Mon.-Sat.
Spanish music and dance show followed by international 'spectacular'.

COMTE MAL Son Termens, Bunyola.
• Opens 2030. Dinner and show 2100.
Wenches serve a medieval banquet. Knights joust and frolic.

SON AMAR Ctra Palma-Soller (10.8km).
• 2015 Mon.-Sat. (Summer), 2015 Wed & Sat. (Winter).
Barbecue, folk-dancing and top of the bill entertainers of yesteryear.

PIRATE ADVENTURE Ctra La Porrasa, Magalluf.
• 2000-2400 Wed., Thurs. & Sun. (English), Sat. (Spanish) Apr.-Jan.;
2000-2400 Sun (English and Spanish) Feb.-Mar.
Caribbean atmosphere. Noisy pirates aboard mock-up ship. Plenty of audience participation. Prizes. Ends with dancing.

ES MAL LLOC Ctra Muro-Ca'n Picafort.
• 1200 Thur. and Sun.. Summer - also at 2000.
Barbecue and as much fun as you make it.

LA PONDEROSA Crta S'Horta, Felanitx.
• 2000 Wed. (May-Sept.).
'Western'-style barbecue and entertainment.

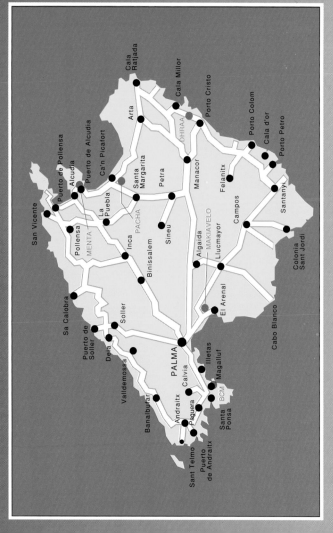

Discos

There's no shortage of these late-night venues in the restorts. Many hotels and apartments complexes have their own. See **NIGHTLIFE, Palma.**

BCM
Av S'Olivera, Magalluf.
Futuristic mega-disco with capacity for 5,000. Truly out of this world and only the famous 'Ku' in Ibiza can compare. Latest sound, light and TARM laser equipment. Five video screens. Concerts by top international stars. Below, the Royale Night Club is totally different - dance bands play nostalgic tunes and grupos rocieros *accompany sevillanas. Also a restaurant serving pizzas and international dishes.*

DHRAA
Ctra Porto Cristo-Cala Millor.
Unusual, attractively designed nightspot. Indoors or under the stars. Good international music.

MAKIAVELO
Playa de Palma.
Music selection with nostalgia for the 60s and 70s. Orchestra. Special events at weekends. More tourists at Kiss (Ca'n Pastilla) and Zorba's (El Arenal).

MENTA
Av Tucán, Puerto de Alcudia.
Reputation for always having the very latest international sounds. Go to Casablanca for Arabian Nights decor and live music.

PACHA
Ctra de Santa Margarita, Ca'n Picafort.
Terrace, garden and pleasant disco for 1,000. Mostly Spanish nightbirds. Nearby, Rojo Disco is much more a foreigners' favourite.

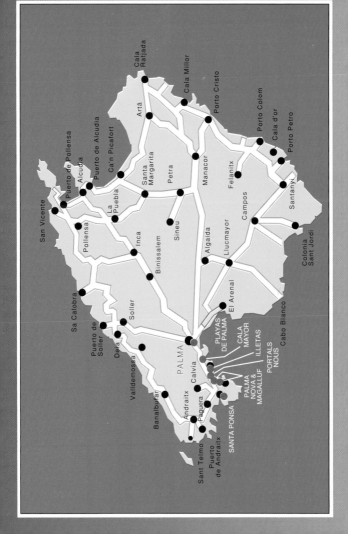

PLAYAS DE PALMA
Including Cala Gamba, Ca'n Pastilla, El Arenal, Cala Blava.
These purpose-built resorts of high-rise accommodation, average eating places and many bars and discos stretch along nearly 5 km of beach.

PALMA
Including El Terreno, Son Vida.
The beach resorts along Bahía de Palma are within easy reach of the city. Son Vida is a smart inland urban district with excellent sports facilities. El Terreno has plenty of lively places for eating, drinking and nightlife.

CALA MAYOR TO PAGUERA
Along the scenic coast, south west of Palma, there is a continuous ribbon development of modern resorts which operate all year. See **RESORTS 2.**

CALA MAYOR
Including San Agustín, Ca's Català.
Spain's Royal Family have their summer holiday home on the northern promontory of this cala. *The long sandy beach has good amenities.*

ILLETAS
With Portals Nous, this resort is regarded as more up-market than others along this stretch of coast. Illetas has the best facilities and gets crowded.

PORTALS NOUS
Including Costa de Bendinat, Costa d'en Blanes.
Includes a narrow strip of sandy beach as well as rocky areas with coves of shingle or sand beaches.

PALMA NOVA AND MAGALLUF
Bustling and brash, these two resorts epitomize the mass tourism for which Majorca is best known. Two wide bays with golden sand beaches.

SANTA PONSA
Set on the scoop of a bay with a background of low hills, this resort has rapidly acquired the mini-Miami look but the pace is less hectic.

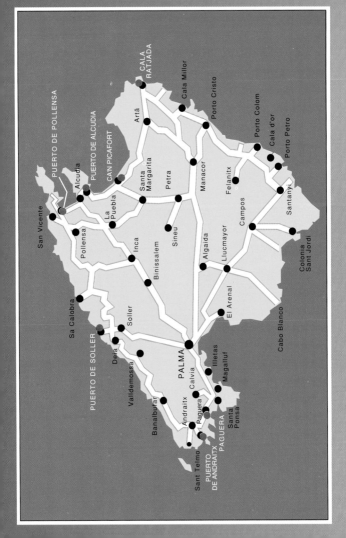

PAGUERA
Some old buildings still line the seafront of this relatively new, quite compact resort surrounded by pinewoods. The busy Andratx/Palma road separates the heart of the resort from its four good, sandy beaches.

PUERTO DE ANDRATX
Including Camp de Mar, San Telmo.
The identity of this small fishing village has not yet been lost although it is now a favourite among the yachting fraternity and has attracted the holiday industry. Nightlife is what you make it in simple bars, cafes and restaurants.

PUERTO DE SOLLER
Picturesque port where a palm-fringed beach of sand and shingle is backed by a promenade and a string of simple eating and drinking places.

PUERTO DE POLLENSA
Including Cala San Vicente, Formentor.
From tiny hostals and purpose-built 'package' hotels to the grandness of the renowned Hotel Formentor, there's a wide choice of places to stay in an area that attracts a mix of ages and nationalities.

PUERTO DE ALCUDIA
Including Playas de Mallorca.
Most of the popular bars and restaurants crowd around the old harbour. For about 4 km to the east, lining the curve of the bay and the beach of white sand, are the modern blocks of hotels and the flashier nightspots.

CA'N PICAFORT
Although unimaginatively designed, this modern resort along the middle stretch of Alcudia bay does cater particularly well for family holidays.

CALA RATJADA
Including Cala de sa Font, Cala Guya.
Development has been well-controlled on this beautiful piece of coast. Cala Ratjada retains the charm of an active fishing port. There are ample sports facilities and all types of beach, rock or sand , busy or secluded.

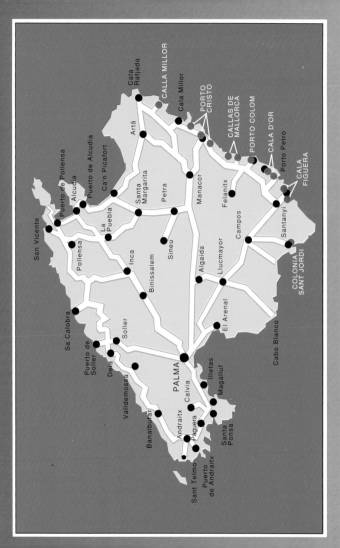

Cala Millor - Sant Jordi

CALA MILLOR
Including Cala Bona, Costa de los Pinos, Playa de Canyamel.
High-rise blocks of hotels, apartments and other amenities catering for a mass market are closely packed right on a 1.5 km stretch of fine sand beach which is well serviced. The summer scene here can be very hectic.

PORTO CRISTO
Inc. S'Illot, Cala Moreya, Sa Coma, Porto Cristo Novo, Cala Estany.
Historically the port for Manacor, Porto Cristo has developed as a small-scale resort. Day trippers to the Caves of Drac and Ham make the otherwise charming and picturesque village very crowded during high-season.

CALAS DE MALLORCA
From Cala Magrana to Cala Murada.
Purpose-built holiday complex of big hotels and apartments on a barren headland. A number of sandy coves backed by cliffs.

PORTO COLOM
Including Cala Marsal.
Bright, little houses line the waterfront of this active fishing village. Its large protected bay has few beaches but is perfect for watersports.

CALA D'OR
Including Porto Petro.
One of the island's larger new resorts. Also one of its most attractive. It's set around a number of pine-fringed coves with small sandy beaches.

CALA FIGUERA
Including Cala Santany.
The hotels and apartments which are going up around here won't encroach on the narrow inlet which this picturesque and busy fishing village hugs. To the south are some of the island's loveliest, unspoilt coves.

COLÓNIA SANT JORDI
Another small village and port where the facilities are low-key, but developing. A long stretch of fine sand fringed by pines, dunes and reeds.

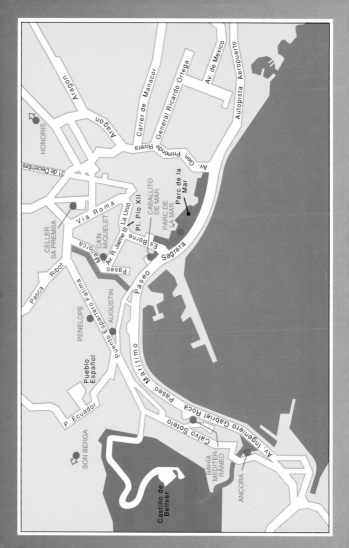

Palma

PARC DE LA MAR Parc de la Mar.
•Budget - Moderate. *View of the cathedral. Speciality is paella.*

CABALLITO DE MAR Pl Lonja/Paseo Sagrera.
•Moderate. *Try one of the* pescado a la sal. *Terrace with view of La Llotja.*

CA'N MIQUELET Galerías Jaime III.
•Budget. *Good* tapas *menu of favourite Majorcan dishes. Good quality.*

CELLER SA PREMSA Pl Obispo Berenguer de Palou 8.
•Closed Sat. & Sun. •Budget.
Big and usually bustling with locals and tourists. Basic Majorcan fare.

AUGUSTÍN San Magin 2.
•Closed Sun. nights. •Budget.
Mediterranean menu of grilled meats, fish and spit-roasted chicken.

PENELOPE Pl Progreso 19.
• Closed Sat. lunch. •Moderate.
Shellfish and fish specialities. Pleasant decor includes art shows.

HONORIS Camino Viejo de Bunyola 76.
•Moderate (lunch) •Expensive (dinner).
Smart service in elegant rooms or lovely garden. Different evening menu presents modern Mediterranean cuisine. Highly recommended.

SON BERGA Ctra de Palma (via Son Dureta), Genova.
•Moderate. *Good, traditional fare in converted farm buildings.*

BAHÍA MEDITERRÁNEO Paseo Marítimo 33.
•Expensive. *Very elegant dining. Well-chosen international dishes perfectly prepared and presented. Turbot in champagne is a speciality.*

ANCORA Ca'n Barbara, Paseo Maritimo.
•Closed Sun., Mon. lunch. •Moderate.
Good choice of meat and fish. Pleasant terrace above small fishing port.

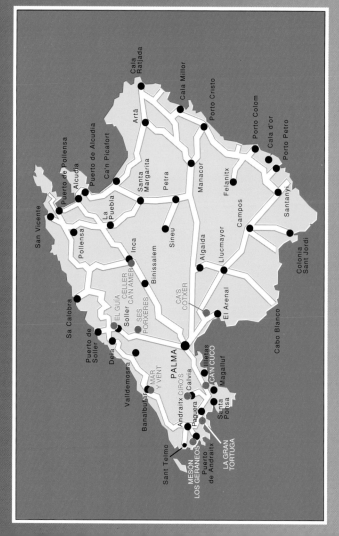

CA'S COTXER Ctra de Arenal 31, Playa de Palma.
•Moderate. *Always busy but attentive. Wide-ranging menu, mainly seafood.*
Interesting combinations like lobster with rabbit.

CIRO'S Paseo de Mar 3, Palma Nova.
•Moderate. *Smart and airy with views across the bay. Mediterranean menu*
of pizzas, meats and seafoods.

CA'N CUCO Av de Palma 14, Calvia.
•Closed Mon. and for lunch in Jul. & Aug. •Budget.
Plain and simple, local favourite for good-value Majorcan food.

LA GRAN TORTUGA Ctra Cala Fornells, Paguera.
•Closed Mon. •Moderate.
Stylish decor and service. Terrace and swimming pool. International menu.

MESÓN LOS GERÁNEOS Av Mateo Bosch 4, Puerto de Andratx.
•Moderate. *Majorcan decor and cooking. List of island and Spanish wines.*

MAR Y VENT Banyalbufar.
•1800-2100. •Moderate (3 courses).
Memorable home-cooking in this delightful family-run hotel. No choice of
main course, selection of starters and desserts. All traditional fare.

SES PORXERES Ctra Palma-Soller, Bunyola.
•Closed Sun night, Mon. & Aug. •Moderate.
Converted barn where a professional team presents grilled meat and game
cooked the Catalan way.

EL GUIA Castanyer (near station), Soller.
•Budget. *Dining room of small hotel serves big helpings of Majorcan food*
for the famished. Daily special is a good bet.

CELLER CA'N AMER Pau 39, Inca.
•Closed Sat. & Sun. (Jun.-Sep.). •Budget.
Typical of the town's traditional cellers.

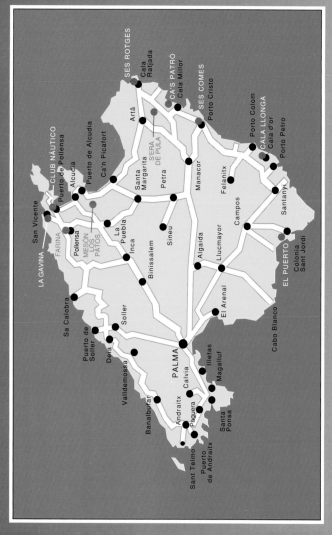

East

LA GAVINA Temporal s/n, Cala San Vicente.
•Moderate. *High standard cuisine in a 1930s setting. Seafood specialities.*

FARINA Pedro Vives 72, Pollensa.
•Moderate. *Tastefully converted grain mill. Innovative combinations like salmon with honey. Follow the chef's suggestions.*

CLUB NÁUTICO Muelle Viejo, Puerto Pollensa.
•Moderate. *Fresh fish and shellfish on the wharf. Terrace with grand views.*

MESÓN LOS PATOS Ctra Sa Pobla-Alcudia (via La Albufera), Alcudia. •Closed Tues.• Moderate.
Pato *(duck) is a speciality. Also fresh fish from its own boat. Charmingly rustic with lively Majorcan clientele. Terrace and swimming pool.*

SES ROTGES Alsedo, Cala Ratjada.
•Closed Nov.-Mar. •Moderate.
Caring conversion of farmhouse into congenial hotel and restaurant. Enjoys high reputation for its French and local cuisine. Terrace.

S'ERA DE PULA Ctra Son Servera-Cala Ratjada, Son Servera.
•1220-1530, 1800-2400. Closed Mon. •Moderate.
Converted farmhouse. Fresh fish depending on the market.

CA'S PATRO Av Antonio Garau 15, Cala Bona, Cala Millor.
•Moderate. *Small, friendly and very popular. Simple cooking, mainly fish.*

SES COMES Av de los Pinos, Porto Cristo.
•Closed Mon. •Budget.
Rape marinera *is one recommendation in this unpretentious eatery.*

CALA LLONGA Av Cala Llonga (facing marina), Cala D'Or.
•Moderate. *Modern, spacious. Seafood specialist but good meats selection.*

EL PUERTO Colonia de Sant Jordi.
•Moderate. *Superb paellas and fresh fish dishes for local regulars.*

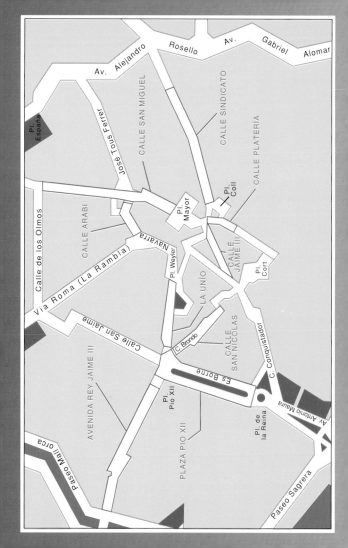

AVENIDA REY JAIME III
The town's smartest shopping street with all types of quality retailers. Midway, there's a big branch of Galerías, Majorca's only department store.

PLAZA PIO XII
For clothing, there is a branch of the C&A chain. Good shops for pearls, leather and suede,and jewellery. Down Paseo Borne you will find straw articles, embroidery, and perfume.

CALLE SAN NICOLAS
In the Barrio Antiguo's cluster of many small streets where you'll enjoy getting lost. Good charcuterie, sweets, espadrilles, wines and spirits.

CALLE JAIME III
Modern clothes boutiques and old-time speciality shops. Fascinating fans and umbrellas at Segura Arrecio. Across the street, a good place for gloves and haberdashery.

CALLE PLATERÍA
Almost every shop is a jeweller, eager to sell. Old and modern pieces.

CALLE SINDICATO
Many low-priced bazaars. Exotic smells in spice shops where saffron is a good buy. Shoes, woven-straw items.

CALLE SAN MIGUEL
New spectacles from opticians, shoes, embroidery work, charcuterie, family clothing, woven straw goods, ceramics and glass.

CALLE ARABI
Antique shops. More in nearby streets.

LA UNIÓ
Shoes, sports gear, toys, Lladró porcelain, pastries. In Pl Santa Catalina Tomás, behind its pretty front of Forn d'es Teatre, a shop selling pastries. Elsewhere, iron and steel Toledo ware.

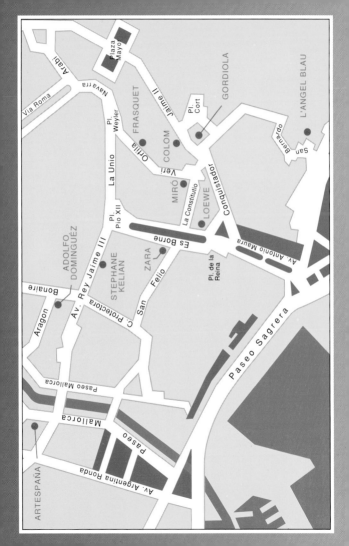

Gifts

ADOLFO DOMÍNGUEZ
Bonaire 7.
Fashions for men and women from Spain's internationally famous designer.

LOEWE
Paseo Borne 2.
High-quality leather and suede clothes, accessories, perfume.

ZARA
Paseo Borne 25.
Big store selling young-style fashionable clothes at moderate prices.

STEPHANE KELIAN
Av Rey Jaime III 16.
Fashionable footwear by acclaimed designers.

MIRÓ
Pl del Rosario 11.
Wide range of jewellery. Smart shop with attentive service.

ARTESPAÑA
Paseo de Mallorca 17.
Selection of some of the best design and craft items from all over Spain.

GORDIOLA
Victoria 2.
Big showroom of glassware. Blown-glass for which Palma is famous.

L'ANGEL BLAU San Bernardo 1.
Ceramics and a wide selection of other craft items.

COLOM Santo Domingo 5.
Epicurean delights, groceries, fresh fruit and vegetables.

FRASQUET Orfila 4.
Chocolates and other sweets. Nice ideas for take-home gifts.

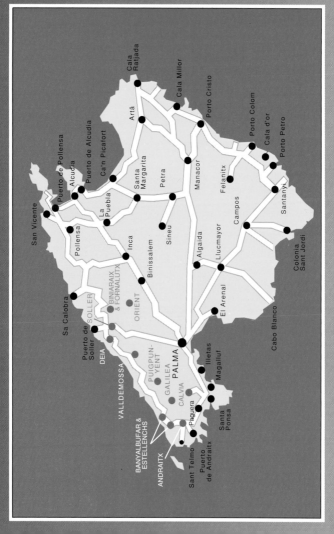

TOWNS & VILLAGES 1

ANDRATX
Set in a valley of farmland and orchard gardens, its Wednesday market is a focus for visitors to the resorts in the southwestern tip of the island.

BANYALBUFAR AND ESTELLENCHS
Banyalbufar is the prettier of these villages where orchards fill wide terraces.

BINIARAIX AND FORNALUTX
Terraces of citrus orchards surround these two hideaway hamlets of steep, cobbled streets and rustic buildings. Expansive views.

CALVIA
The municipal town for the string of resorts south west of Palma.

DEIA
There's a timeless air about this haven of narrow, cobbled streets and flower-bedecked walls, which not even the day trippers in high season disturb.

GALILEA
Mount Galatzo rises above the village which has become a retreat for artists. Wide vistas from the church square across very pretty countryside.

ORIENT
A twisting mountain road leads to this tiny, picture-postcard place which happily claims to be the island's smallest village.

PUIGPUENT
There are a few fine old houses in the narrow streets of this picturesque village and don't miss seeing the Son Forteza manor.

SOLLER
Market town set among citrus groves below the island's highest peaks.

VALLDEMOSSA
The village of narrow, cobbled streets and some good-looking houses rises up a rugged hill, and is dominated by the monastery of Real Cartuja.

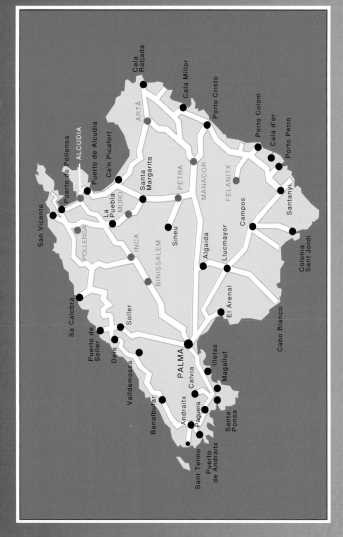

TOWNS & VILLAGES 2

ALCUDIA
Close to the resorts of Alcudia bay, this town gets busy with summer holidaymakers who come to see its old stone walls and narrow streets.

ARTA
The sanctuary of San Salvador dominates this small town of steep and narrow streets. The caves of Arta are 12 km. south east.

BINISSALEM
Main town for the island's wine production. Obvious attractions are its bodegas and shops where the product can be tasted and bought. There are folk-dancing displays in its square.

FELANITX
One of the wine-making towns. Also a centre for ceramic and enamel crafts. Nearby are the sanctuary of San Salvador and Santueri Castle.

INCA
With few pretensions of being attractive, the island's third largest town pulls in many tourists to browse and buy at its leatherwork factories and shops.

MANACOR
Mallorca's second town is a busy place, servicing the east-coast resorts, making artificial pearls, pottery and olivewood items.

MURO
Typical of Es Pla's farming towns, Muro has some fine 17thC houses, one of which is home to a museum displaying island arts and crafts.

PETRA
Birthplace of Junipero Serra, founder of the Californian missions. A small museum honours him.

POLLENSA
Only scrappy remains are evidence of the town's Roman past. It's a dozy place of narrow, winding streets with a quiet plaza.

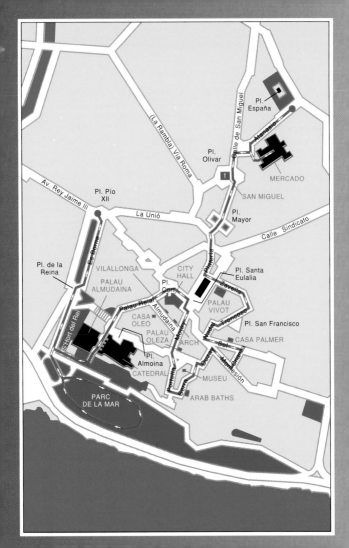

East of Es Borne

2:40 hr. Begin at Pl España. Note the statue of Jaime I (see **A-Z**). Go SW into c/ Padre Atanasio towards Pl Olivar (see **MARKETS**). Exit into c/ San Miguel and turn left. Some good shops. San Miguel church has an impressive altar. Pass into the picturesque Pl Mayor. Shops, bars with outdoor tables, underground bazaar, craft market (see **MARKETS**). 40min. Head along Pl Marqués de Palmer and bear left into c/ Platería, many jewellers. Left into c/ Zavella to look into the Palau Vivot (see **BUILD-INGS-PALMA**). Second right leads to Pl San Francisco. Visit the church and cloister (see **BUILDINGS-PALMA**) and you can't miss the simple statue of Junipero Serra (see **A-Z**) and an American Indian child. 25 min. Into c/ Padre Nadal and left into c/ del Sol to see the solid Casa Palmer (1556) with its Renaissance decoration and upper gallery, a copy of La Llotja's (see **ART GALLERIES, BUILDINGS-PALMA**). Along these narrow streets you'll see more old palaces. Peek into their patios. Right c/ Crianza, right c/ Montesión, left c/ Duzay and across to c/ Serra and the Arab Baths (no. 7) and small, peaceful garden. Continue around into c/ Portella, heart of the Call, once the Jewish district near the old city walls. The Museu de Mallorca is at no. 5 (see **MUSEUMS**). Continue into c/ Morey and stroll into the Palau Oleza's impressive patio. Up on the left across c/ Almudaina, notice an arch from the Arab walls. Enter Pl Santa Eulalia, dominated by its church. The first to be started on Majorca, it has fine external carvings and a high-vaulted Gothic nave. The plaza is a charming, shady place for take refreshment. 45 min. Leave by c/ Cadena into Pl Cort with its handsome city hall (see **BUILD-INGS-PALMA**). Left into c/ Palau Reial. On the left, c/ Almudaina has the Casa Oleo (no. 8), notable patio and staircase, and Casa Vilallonga (no. 13), small Plateresque windows. Continue to Pl Almoina, and admire the cathedral and the Palau Almudaina. See **BUILDINGS-PALMA**. 20 min. On the south side of Pl Almoina, go down the steps to a terrace for a different view of the cathedral and panoramas across the bay. Down more steps to the bronze *hondero* statue (see **A-Z**) of a youth with his sling. Detour to the Parc del Mar, reclaimed from the sea and opened in 1984. Abstract forms by Alfaro and a mural by Miró (see **A-Z**). Back into the S'Hort del Rei gardens of flowers, fountains and cyprus trees. Continue through Pl de la Reina and up the eastern side of Es Borne which has some interesting shops. Finish at Pl Pio XII. 30 min.

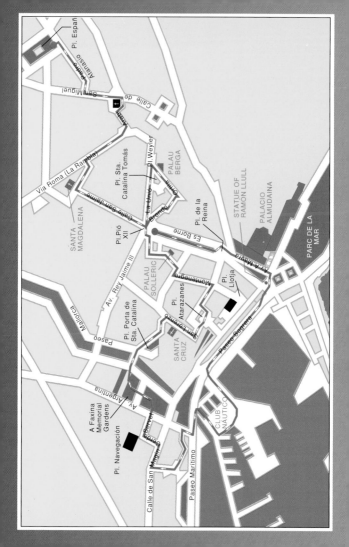

West of Es Borne

2:45 hr. Begin at Pl Pio XII. Go down the centre of Es Borne and along Av Antonio Maura. Statue of Ramón Llull at the end (see **A-Z**). On the left is the Palau Almudaina's Gothic gallery (see **BUILDINGS-PALMA**). Right into Paseo Sagrera, a number of seafood restaurants. Right into Pl Llotja and stop to admire the grand Gothic building (see **ART GALLERIES**, **BUILDINGS-PALMA**). Go in if it's open for an art exhibition. 25 min.
Continue along Paseo Sagrera. Left across Paseo Marítimo to reach the fishing-boat harbour, usually busy with lots of local colour. Stroll along to the contrasting scene of the yacht-filled Club Náutico. 30 min.
Cross the Paseo Marítimo again. Left across Av Argentina and up steps into the district of Es Jonquet with its preserved windmills, many bars and nightspots. On to Pl Vapor, lively neighbourhood focal point. Right c/ San Magín, left c/ Cerda to Pl Navegación and its fresh food market (see **MARKETS**). Right into c/ Servet and across Av Argentina again to the A Faxina memorial garden. 25 min.
Right over a bridge above the Torrente de Riera (dry in summer) and through Pl Porta de Sta Catalina. Note the Baroque portico of Santa Cruz church. Right into old, narrow and sometimes smelly c/ San Lorenzo, then left and through Pl Atarazanes, a working-class gathering place, to c/ Apuntadores. This is a brash street of many bars and varied eating places. Admire the distinctive staircase at no. 51, Casa Marqués. Left into c/ Montenegro. Right to c/ Cayetano (Gaieta) and the Palau Solleric (see **ART GALLERIES**). Go in, if not to view the modern art, at least to see the elegantly proportioned patio and gallery, probably Palma's finest. Right an alley leads to Pl Pio XII. 35 min.
For just a taste of Palma's shopping delights, cross over to c/ Brondo, leading to c/ San Nicolás and left along c/ Orfila to Pl Sta Catalina Tomás. Note the imposing facade of Palau Berga (law courts). Left along c/ Unió with the Casa Balaguer (see **ART GALLERIES**), and return to Pl Pio XII. 15 min.
Right into c/ San Jaime, an evocative street. Note the Hostal Borne's courtyard (no. 3), art galleries (nos. 6 & 15) and food shop (no. 23). Bar Angel (no. 27) is a pleasant spot to have a drink. Right by Santa Magdalena church to reach La Rambla. Right down this shaded paseo with its flower stalls. Left at c/ Arabi (antique shops). Left into c/ San Miquel, right through Pl Olivar. Finish at Pl España. 35 min.

Estellencs

Accommodation: Majorca has Europe's densest concentration of holiday accommodation. For instance, it offers more beds in hotels and apartments than the whole of Greece. Only a few places have so far aimed at the top end of the international market and in this category the Hotel Formentor is the most outstanding. There are some delightful, family-run establishments.

Officially rated accommodation: Hotels -H- one to five star with *Gran Lujo* the very top rating. A *Hotel Apartamento* -HA- offers full hotel services with accommodation in apartments. A *Hotel Residencia* -HR- does not have a full restaurant. *Hostales* -Hs- are much like hotels, usually with more modest facilities, and are rated one to three stars. *Apartamentos Turísticos* -AT- are rated from one to four keys, have self-catering facilites and usually require a minimum stay of one week. *Fondas* (inns) and *Casas de Huéspedes* (guest houses) offer the most basic accommodation. *Camping* is classified upwards from 3rd to 1st *Categoría*. There are nine *Ciudades de Vacaciones* or Sun Clubs with most accommodation in bungalows, operating from April to October, which have comprehensive sports and entertainment facilities. See also **Camping, Villas and Apartments**.

Airport: Son San Juan airport is 10 km west along the motorway from Palma. Terminal A for scheduled airlines, Terminal B for charter flights. Facilities include: bank, tourist office, hotel booking service, car hire desks, post office, baggage porters, souvenir and duty-free shops, bars. Buses 17-A and 17-B link with the city (15 mins). Metered taxis are relatively inexpensive (supplements for the airport journey and for baggage).

Miscellaneous Information:
Flight Enquiries Tel 26 46 24
Tourist Office   26 08 03
Hotel Desk   26 26 49 (Ultramar Express)

Anglada Camarasa, Hermen: Born Barcelona 1871; died Majorca 1959. One of the leading lights among the second generation of modernista painters who showed a new approach to colour, brush-work and form, and whose subjects dealt with social deprivation. In his landscapes, colour strikingly dominates form. He had lived and painted in Barcelona, Paris and Valencia before settling in Pollensa.

Atalaya: Watchtowers along the coast from which warnings of approaching pirates and invaders were given. Ses Animas, between Estellencs and Banyalbufar, is a popular example.

Babysitters: Many hotel and apartment complexes operate a day-time care and entertainment programme and a room listening service at night. In some small places a member of the family or staff may babysit. You can also ask locally about *canguros*, professional babysitters, and *guarderías*, crèches.

Beaches: There are no 'undiscovered' beaches on the island. The most secluded, good beaches are in the NE and SE, reached on foot or by boat. Except during freak conditions, the popular beaches are all very safe with little tidal variation. The waters within Palma bay can become unpleasantly polluted. See **BEACHES, RESORTS.**

Best Buys: Leather and suede clothing, footwear and accessories should be a good buy, but more likely so in Palma's shops than in the 'factories' or markets. Simple strings of artificial pearls are a good buy. A few pearls in an elaborate expensive setting are probably not. Embroidered linen goods, woven-grass items, simple ceramics, cleverly carved olivewood and inexpensive paintings by local artists are among the best buys to consider.

Bicycle and Motorcycle Hire: Hire facilities are widely available in the resorts. Check that your holiday insurance does not exclude cover of any accidents while riding one of these. Minimum age for mopeds is 16; for motorcycles over 75cc it's 18. Crash helmet required for latter, recommended for both.

Birdwatching: The island enjoys a reputation among ornithologists and amateur birdwatchers for its variety of resident and migratory birdlife. Specialist operators offer holidays in resorts near the Albufera marshlands along Alcudia bay where the birdlife is richest. The salt flats

Cala D'Or

of Salines de Levante, near Colònia de Sant Jordi, also attract birds.

Blauets: Blue-cassocked boys from the Augustinian monks' music and choir school at Lluc. They usually sing at noon and sunset.

Bullfighting: Its aficionados regard the performance as an art form, a ritualized ballet in which the lurking danger to the man heightens the intensity. The fate of the toro is always the same. Palma's Plaza de Toros Monumental has corridas on Sunday afternoons in summer. Coach excursions from most resorts. Bullrings at Inca and Muro are used less frequently. Children under 15 are not admitted.

Buses: Comprehensive network of scheduled bus services from Palma to most towns and resorts, and connecting between the resort areas, provides an inexpensive means of getting around. Most services operate from Palma's Pl España, or nearby streets. Other principal stops at Pl Pío XII (Illetas), Pl Reina (Playa de Palma), La Rambla (Andraitx). More information from hotels, tourist offices and Pl España. Routes and schedules are also displayed at bus stops.

Cala Blava: See **Playas de Palma**.

Cala Bona: See **Cala Millor**.

Cala de sa Font: See **Cala Ratjada**.

Cala d'Or: This large, new and attractive resort is especially popular with Scandinavian tourists. Most of its buildings succesfully blend modern and traditional design and many follow the simple Ibizan style. The range of accommodation, sports and entertainments is comprehensive and the resort caters well for younger people and active families. It is considered that it contain the east coast's best selection of shops, restaurants and nightspots. In the pretty fishing port of Porto Petro there's a contrasting choice of simpler accommodation and places to eat. Nearby Cala Mondragó has a large, inviting beach of fine sand. OIT Av Cala Longa. See **RESORTS 3**.

Cala Estany: See **Porto Cristo**.

Cala Figuera: It's offerings of man-made holiday facilities are mostly limited to a few modest places to stay and eat. The fishing village itself retains a certain traditional charm. Further to the south are some of the island's loveliest, unspoilt coves. Calas Santanyi and Llombards have facilities, others have none and can only be reached by foot or boat. See **RESORTS: CALA MILLOR-SANT JORDI**.

Cala Gamba: See **Playas de Palma**.

Cala Guya: See **BEACHES**, **Cala Ratjada**.

Cala Marsal: See RESORTS: CALA MILLOR-SANT JORDI.

Cala Mayor: The large establishments purpose-built for the package holiday industry predominate along this stretch of coastline to the south west of Palma. However, accommodation is still available in hotels and apartments of all classes and in villas, chalets and bungalows. The majority of shops, bars, eating places and nightlife venues cater largely for young foreign holidaymakers who don't want to spend too much and prefer the food and drink they have at home. Many of the small businesses are foreign owned. Good facilities for healthy fun are available at numerous sports clubs, pleasure marinas and watersports centres. It's easy to move between the resorts by road or on boat excursions. Cala Mayor includes the resorts of San Agustín and Ca's Català and the OIT office is at Ctr Andraitx, Ca's Català, tel: 40 27 39. See RESORTS: PALMA-SANTA PONSA.

Cala Millor: A highly-developed tourist resort area. In high season the pace here can be as hectic as that in the big resorts around Palma Bay. It is much quieter at the Cala Bona end, where there's a small fishing port with watersports and three artificial coves. Costa de los Pinos is an exclusive development with luxury villas, golf courses and top-class hotels. Playa de Canyamel, lined with pines and protected by cliffs, is being developed with discretion. OIT Fetjet Parc de la Mar. See RESORTS: CALA MILLOR-SANT JORDI.

Cala Moreya: See Porto Cristo.

Cala Ratjada: Many of the villas, hotels and restaurants have idyllic settings along this attractive stretch of coastline. Modern developments have been well controlled so that that attractiveness is not lost. There are all types of beaches: in Cala Ratjada, shingle and rocks of the central bathing area or the sand and rocks of Playa Son Moll, and rocky Cala Cat; Cala Guya with fine sand, dunes and shade; Cala de sa Font's two tiny coves of fine, soft sand. Capdepera, Arta, Cuevas de Arta (see CAVES) and prehistoric remains are interesting places to visit. OIT office is on Pl deis Mariners. See RESORTS: PAGUERA-CALA RATJADA.

Cala San Vicente: See **Puerto de Pollensa**.

Cala Santanyi: See **Cala Figuera**.

Calas de Majorca: See RESORTS: CALA MILLOR-SANT JORDI.

Camp de Mar: See **Puerto de Andraitx**.

Camping: Both official sites are in the north: Camping Platja Blava, Playa de Muro, tel: 53 78 63 (1st Category); Club San Pedro, Colonia San Pedro, tel: 28 90 23 (3rd Category). Off-site camping is not encouraged and is never allowed on beaches, in mountain areas or along dry river beds. Always ask permission from private owners.

Ca'n Pastilla: See **Playas de Palma**.

Ca'n Picafort: This resort, although well-supplied with amenities, is not the most attractive of the island's recent developments. The serviced main beach is long and narrow with white sand and occasional rocks. Son Baulo beach has coarser sand, dunes and some shade. The more tranquil Playas de Muro (see BEACHES) have a layer of small shells on soft sand. Excursions include trips in glass-bottomed boats to a tiny island with prehistoric remains.
OIT office is on Pl Gabriel Roca. See RESORTS: PAGUERA-CALA RATJADA.

Car Hire: All the big international firms operate in Majorca, either directly or with Spanish associates. Scheduled airlines offer 'fly-drive' schemes. Holiday operators have car-hire offers. Smaller, local firms whose leaflets may also be picked up at hotels and tourist offices, usually have lower rates. Check if your hotel has any special arrangements. It is worthwhile looking out for special deals and term discounts. Don't forget to compare all-inclusive costs as insurance and mileage charges can bump up the bill considerably. Insurance includes third party and a bail bond but it is also advisable to take comprehensive insurance including collision damage waiver. Remember value added tax is 12%. See **Motoring**.

Ca's Català: See **Cala Mayor**.

Catalan Language: This distinct language, which looks like an amalgam of Spanish and French in written form but sounds more like Portuguese when spoken, began developing out of Provençal from the 7thC onwards. It is now the native language of about seven million people, spoken with local variations in Catalunya, Valencia, the Balearic Islands, Andorra and the eastern French Pyrenees. Since the end of Franco's dictatorship and the gaining of regional autonomy, Catalan and its Mallorquín dialect have once again flourished.

Caves: There are many *cuevas* on the island. In times past they have been used for religous rites, as hiding places from invaders, and as smugglers' caches. Not all have been explored and only a few have been developed as tourist attractions. See **CAVES**.

Children: Like most Mediterranean people, Majorcans display their fondness and tolerance of children. They're made very welcome almost anywhere and at any time. Beyond the safe, sandy beaches there are many enjoyable distractions and opportunities for children to practise favourite sports or try something new. See **CHILDREN**.

Chopin, Frédéric (1810-1849): In the winter of 1835, the Polish composer rented rooms at what had been Valldemossa's monastery where he spent about three months with the French author, George Sand (Aurora Dupin), and her two children. As she recorded in her book, *Un Hiver en Majorque*, they had a rather miserable time, liking very little of what they found. Ironically, much fuss is still made about the unremarkable fact that Chopin visited the island.

Cigarettes and Tobacco: Smoking materials are sold in an *estanco* (*tabacos*). Many have a selection of international brands. Spanish cigarettes are either *negro* (black) and strong, such as Ducados, or *rubio* (blond) and mild, like Fortuna. Well-made, strong or mild cigars from the Canaries are relatively inexpensive. Pipe tobaccos are mostly coarse and strong.

Pueblo Español, Palma

Cinema: Spain has an active and adventurous film industry. Most foreign films are dubbed. Showings in original version with Spanish subtitles are advertised as 'v.o.'. First showing in Palma's cinemas is usually at 1530, last at 2230. Check for cinema shows in tourist complexes.

Climate: The mild Mediterranean climate is favourably affected by local features. Sea breezes modify heat and humidity at the height of summer. Relatively high, westerly mountains protect the south from the colder winter winds. Waters along shallow beaches are quickly heated by the sun. Because the island has a varied landscape, there's a noticeable variation in a day's weather from place to place. If it's too hot and sultry by the sea, you'll find that a short journey away the mountains will be cool and shady. If it's cloudy on the north coast, it may well be sunny along the south, and vice versa. In Palma temperatures seldom exceed 36°C or drop below 5°C. Its average temperature and rainfall are: spring 23.6°C, 34mm; summer 30.3°C, 54mm; autumn 21°C, 85mm; winter 16°C, 120mm. There is sunshine on about 300 days of each year.

Colonia de Sant Jordi: The island's only spa hotel is nearby. The beaches of Trenc,Ses Covetes and La Rapita are popular with islanders on summer weekends. Desolate Cabrera island can be visited on day trips. OIT Doctor Barraquer. See **RESORTS: CALA MILLOR-SANT JORDI**.

Columbus, Christopher: In 1992, Majorca, like the rest of Spain and much of the world, will celebrate the quincentenary of Christopher Columbus's first voyage to the Americas. Little credence is given to the island fable that the explorer (known locally as Cristobal Colón) was born in Genova, now a suburb of Palma, or near Santueri.

Complaints: Places of accommodation, restaurants and petrol stations have to keep a *hoja de reclamación* (complaints forms in triplicate). If your complaint is about price, you must first pay the bill before requesting the forms. After the form is filled in one copy is retained by you, another is sent to the tourism department of the regional government. This is a valuable consumer-protection facility which should not

Cuevas

be abused by using it for petty complaints. You can notify tourist offices of complaints although they may not always be able to do anything to help you directly.

Consulates: **United Kingdom** Pl Mayor 3D, 71 24 45 **United States of America** Av Jaime III 26, 72 26 60.

Conversion Charts:

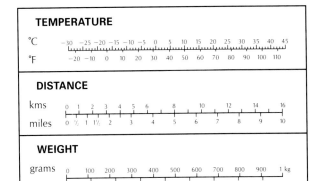

TEMPERATURE

°C −30 −25 −20 −15 −10 −5 0 5 10 15 20 25 30 35 40 45

°F −20 −10 0 10 20 30 40 50 60 70 80 90 100 110

DISTANCE

kms 0 1 2 3 4 5 6 8 10 12 14 16

miles 0 ½ 1 1½ 2 3 4 5 6 7 8 9 10

WEIGHT

grams 0 100 200 300 400 500 600 700 800 900 1 kg

ounces 0 4 8 12 1 lb 20 24 28 2 lb

Costa de Bendinat: See RESORTS 1 - Portals Nous.

Costa de los Pinos: See Cala Millor.

Costa d'en Blanes: See RESORTS 1 - Portals Nous.

Courtesies: Remember you are a guest in another country. It is discourteous to ignore its rules of behaviour and very foolhardy to break its laws. Tourists often cause offence by not dressing and behaving with respect when visiting religious buildings. Generally, Majorcans are extremely tolerant of foreigners' different ways and manners. Two essential phrases: *por favor* (please) and *gracias* (thank you). Going into a room, shop, *etc* or when formally meeting people, the greeting is *buenos días* (good day) or *buenas tardes* (good afternoon and evening). Leaving, it's *adiós* or *buenas noches* (goodnight). A much used phrase is *de nada* (you're welcome).

Crime: Compared with many cities and resort areas, the level of crime against tourists is very low in Majorca. Perhaps, because it's an island and the criminal element can be more easily contained. Some advice: deposit valuables in the hotel or apartment safe; ensure that your hotel room, apartment or villa is securely locked when you leave; carry the least possible amount of cash; take care about flashing cash around and when leaving a bank; carry handbags and cameras on the off-street side; don't wear jewellery; avoid lonely places; walk with a friend or in a group; don't leave anything in sight in a car; use licensed taxis at night; be alert, and, importantly, show that you are. If you or a friend have been the subject of a crime, try to find witnesses and report the incident to the police immediately. Make sure to get a copy of your statement for insurance purposes.

Customs:

Duty paid into:	Cigarettes	Cigars	Tobacco	Spirits	Wine
Spain	**300**	**75**	**400g**	**1.5l**	**5l**
U.K.	**300**	**75**	**400g**	**1.5l**	**5l**

Dentists: see **Medical Treatment.**

Palma

Disabled: Helpful facilities are limited, toilets especially. Make full enquiries at travel agents or holiday operators before booking.

Drinks: Although tap water is safe, foreigners usually fare better by sticking to *agua mineral, con gas* or *sin gas,* which is bottled mineral water, still or carbonated. *Te* (tea) is usually served *con limón*, with a slice of lemon. *Infusión de manzanilla* is refreshing camomile tea. *Horchata* is a milk-like drink made from ground nuts. *Granizado* is iced, fresh fruit juice. *Café solo* (black) or *café con leche* (with milk). Chocolate, thick and creamy, is drunk for breakfast or a nightcap. Various qualities of Spanish and imported beer, *cerveza*, are available.

Una caña (draught beer) is usually lower priced. *Sangria* is of varying strength and is made from ice, soda-water, red wine, brandy, fruit and juices. *Cava* is good-quality sparkling wine, usually at reasonable prices. Sherry is called *Jerez* - *fino* (pale dry), *amontillado* (medium), *oloroso* (heavier and sweeter). *Coñac* (brandy) varies from rough to fine (10 year or older *reservas*). *Palo*, flavoured with crushed almond shells is one of the island's many liqueurs. See **Wines.**

Drugs: Possession of drugs is illegal and bringing drugs into the country is subject to harsh penalties. Previously liberal policies have hardened to prevent drugs, and the associated crime, becoming a problem.

El Arenal: See **Playas de Palma**.

Electricity: 220/225 volt. Round-pin, two-point plugs. Wiring is colour-coded to international standard. Older buildings may have 110/125 volt supplies.

El Terreno: See RESORTS: PALMA-SANTA PONSA.

Emergencies: Dial 091 for the Policia Nacional. Concentrate on giving your location, nature of emergency and saying what other services may be required.

Fauna: You won't encounter any dangerous animals. The few snakes are not poisonous. The litle, lizard-like gecko is harmless, so don't kill it. Mosquitoes are the only things likely to cause any bother but you can take precautions against them. On warm evenings you'll hear the chirping cicadas. Hares, rabbits, and game birds are shot for the pot from October to January. The wild mountain goats are protected.

Ferries: Regular connections with Palma throughout the year: Ibiza (0630), Barcelona (0800), Valencia (0900), Mahón (Menorca) (0600). May-Oct.: daily hydrojet to Ibiza. June-Sept.: connections with Sete (France). Nov.-Mar.: connections with Genoa (Italy) and the Canary Islands. Miscellaneous information: Compañia Transmediterránea, Muelle Viejo 5, Palma. Tel.: 72 67 40.

Fiestas: Only Palma's Semana Santa processions, notably on Maundy Thursday, compare with the mainland's many spectacular events but hardly a week goes by without a fiesta somewhere on the island. Some are purely traditional, others have become occasions to play modern music very loudly in public places. Medieval *cavallets* (dressed as horses) and *cossiers* (in other disguises) dance in many of the traditional parades. Mock battles between *moros i cristians* are another theme. Bonfires and fireworks are often the central feature.

Fiestas attracting larger crowds include: *Carro Triunfal* - Valldemossa, 28 July, an allegorical procession celebrating one of the island's favourite saints, Santa Catalina Tomás; *Festa de'es Vermar* - Binissalem, last Sunday of September and into October, wine festival, merry-making and folklore displays; *Dijous Bo* - Inca, 'Good Thursday' mid-November, agricultural fair, parades, dancing, competitions.

Fishing: Enquire at local tourist offices about licences, the best spots for rock fishing, organized trips, boat and tackle hire. Sole, sea bass, denton, dorado, seabream are some varieties. Reservoirs of Gorg Blau and Cuber have trout and carp.

Flamenco: Four separate talents are expressed in a full performance: *cante* (singing), *baile* (dancing), *toque* (guitar playing) and *jaleo* (rhythmic clapping and footwork). The best performers are said to have *duende*, an undefinable quality. *Flamenco jondo*, profound and melancholic, expresses the deepest emotions. Light and lively *flamenco chico* is more about sensual love and sadnesses overcome. Commercial *tablaos* usually present a popularized mix of the two.

Flora: Amateur botanists will be delighted with the variety and accessibility of the island's wild plants - over 1500 types of shrubs, heathers, wild herbs and bright spring flowers. Pines and holm oaks are the most plentiful trees. Annual harvests are taken from the many olive trees, some very old and gnarled, carobs with their heavy seed pods, almond trees which produce a spectacular display of pinky-white blossom in February (as well as producing 70% of Spain's crop) and sweet-smelling citrus trees (mostly in the Soller valley). Figs and apricots are also widely grown.

Folklore: Performances at tourist venues can be somewhat jaded. You will find more genuine traditions and spontaneity from dancers

and musicians at one of the fiestas. Dances of courtship, the *bolero*, *jota* and *parado* are accompanied by varying combinations of bagpipes, fife and drum, guitars and castanets. A white lace headscarf and full, brightly-striped black skirt are distinctive items of the woman's costume, the baggy breeches of the man's.

Food and Eating Places: Fast-food and take-away places of every description are plentiful. Local specialities provide more memorable snacks and meals.

Ensaimada, light, fluffy pastry, sometimes filled with cream, almonds or a preserve, eaten for breakfast and as a dessert; *coco,* like a small pizza and filled with vegetable, fish or something sweet; *empanada,* meat and vegetable pie; *sobrasada,* seasoned and aged pork sausage, delicious on *pan payés,* simple bread; *pa amb oli,* bread spread with fresh tomato, seasoned with salt and olive oil.

Sopas mallorquinas, thick soups of vegetables and sliced bread, sometimes pork slices and mushrooms are added; *tumbet,* tomato, peppers, aubergine, pumpkin and potato fried in oil; *tremp,* a summer salad of tomato, green pepper and onion; *berenjenas rellenas,* stuffed aubergines; *arroz brut* and *arroz a la marinera*, rice with meat and fish respectively; *paella*, Spain's best-known dish should be served only at lunchtime and cooked to order; *frit de mallorquin*, fried, spiced innards of pork or lamb; *lechona asada*, roast suckling pig is the traditional dish for celebrations; *escaldums*, casserole of chicken or turkey with potato and almonds; *pescado* or *peix*, a choice of many kinds of fish, often best when simply grilled, a la planca; *calderata langosta*, lobster pieces in a thick, tomato-based sauce.

Meal times: breakfast until 1100; lunch 1300-1500; dinner from 2030 (places catering to tourists open earlier). Grading of restaurants, one to five forks, reflects the standards of facilities rather than cooking.

Formentor: See **Puerto de Pollensa**.

Golf: Tourist authorities are encouraging private enterprise to build more golf courses. They see it as a means of upgrading the island's tourism image, attracting higher-spending visitors and employing the tourism infrastructure more fully in winter. It is hoped that within a few years the number will double from the existing nine courses. Most will be in the Calvia area. See **GOLF**.

Hairdressers: A *peluqueria* is where you go. They're plentiful and many are unisex. Prices vary greatly, so check before the stylist gets to work on your *pelo* (hair).

Health Hints: Drinks are inexpensive, measures are generous, and the heat generates a thirst and alcoholic overindulgence is one of the biggest health hazards for foreigners. Sunburn is painful and sunstroke is very dangerous. Pace your exposure to the sun, use high-filter creams for the first few days and wear a hat. Drink one of the bottled waters (*agua mineral*) and stick to it. Avoid having ice, too many salads, mayonnaise and any place whose standards of hygiene looks dubious. If your digestion is feeling the strain, eat simple vegetable dishes, tortillas, chicken or plainly grilled fish. Health foods are available from *herboristerías* in Palma and many resorts. First-aid preparations and patent medicines are sold in *farmacias*.

Honderos: Native troops, armed with slings with which they were deadly accurate, who traditionally fought naked. They could not beat off the Roman invasion in 123 BC, even fighting with Carthage's army, and subsequently gained fame in Roman legions. See the statue of a *hondero* near Palma's cathedral.

Hooliganism: The authorities are clamping down on hooligan behaviour with a new severity. On the spot fines of 5000 pesetas for noise disturbance are being levied. Any foreigner causing damage to property or persons will be arrested and deported or taken to a court whose sentences could include jail terms.

Horseriding: At a Club Hípico or Rancho you'll find horses for hire, riding instruction, group excursions. The best facilities and countryside for convenient, even-ground trekking are at east-coast (Cala D'Or) and north-coast resorts.

Hours: Shops: Mon.-Fri. 0900/1000 -1330/1400 and 1630/1730 -

2000/2100. Sat. half-day. In the high season some shops may stay open later to take advantage of the tourist trade, in winter some close earlier. Galerías department store: Mon.-Sat. 1000-2000. Hypermarkets Mon.-Sat. 1000-2200. Business Offices: Mon.-Fri. 0900-1400 and 1630-1900. Government Offices: Mon.-Fri. 1100-1300. Banks: Mon.-Fri. 0900-1400, Sat. 0900-1300. See **SHOPPING**.

Hypermarkets: The island's two big stores, selling most things from foods to furniture, are both in Palma: PRYCA, c/ General Riera (road to Esporles); CONTINENTE, c/ Cardenal Rossello (off the airport road).

Illetas: Wooded hillsides and rocky promontaries separate three coves with gently sloping beaches of fine sand. See **RESORTS 1.**

Jaime: Jaime I, king of Aragon and Catalunya, who routed Moslem forces on Majorca in 1229, became known as El Conquistador (the Conqueror) and increased individual rights and improved the island's trade. On his death in 1276, his kingdom was divided between two sons and Jaime II received the new crown of Majorca. This Jaime was deposed in1285 by his nephew, Alfonso III of Aragon, but with help from the Pope he resumed his reign in 1298. He established his court in the renovated Almudiana palace, built Bellver Castle and extended the Royal Chapel which became the great cathedral. Franciscans and Dominicans were encouraged to build churches and monasteries. On Es Pla, eleven new towns were built in a programme to improve agriculture. The island's fleet and foreign trade was expanded. Artists and writers had the king's support. Majorca's Golden Age continued under Sancho I (1311-1324) and his nephew Jaime III. In 1343, Pedro IV of Aragon deposed Jaime, uniting the two kingdoms. The exiled king tried to regain his throne but was killed in a battle at Llucmayor in 1349.

Juan Carlos I: The King of Spain was born in 1938, a grandson of Spain's last monarch. In 1962, he married Princess Sofía, daughter of the King of Greece. Franco had named Juan Carlos to be his successor as head of state and when the dictator died in 1975 he was proclaimed King. Juan Carlos set a course steering the country to democracy under a new constitution (1978) which he has stoutly protected. With the Queen and their children, Elena, Cristina and Felipe, he has created a popular and populist monarchy with little of the pomp and protocol surrounding Europe's other crowns. The family take their summer holiday at the Marivent Palace, near Cala Mayor, where members of Europe's other royal houses are frequent guests. On his 18th birthday in January 1986, Prince Felipe became heir apparent.

Language: Castilian Spanish is Spain's official language. Mallorquin, the home language of many islanders, is derived from Catalan (see **Catalan Language**) and its use is being widely promoted. Place names and signs appear in either or both languages which causes some confusion for visitors. Almost everybody you're likely to meet will speak Castilian and in the main tourist areas many islanders speak English, German or French.

Laundries: Hotels have laundry and dry-cleaning services. A *lavandería* (laundry) or *tintorería* (dry cleaner), of which there are many, is likely to be cheaper. They usually charge by weight and need a minimum of 24 hours.

Llauds: Looking like lifeboats from ocean liners, Majorca's typical fishing boats are open craft measuring from 6 to 12 m. They sail at night from the many ports and return at dawn, always hoping to be loaded with fish for which there will be ready buyers on the quay. Often their catch is poor for in-shore fish stocks have declined as a result of over-fishing and pollution.

Llull, Ramón: Born in 1232, the son of a Catalan nobleman who had fought in the Christian reconquest of Majorca, he grew up to be a dissolute courtier. Then, when he was 28, mystical visions persuaded him that his task was to spread the faith. For a time he withdrew to monastic life on Mount Randa but he also travelled widely, gaining an international reputation and with the help of King Jaime II founded a school of Oriental Studies on Majorca. His poems, novels, essays on theology and philosophy were written in Catalan, Provençal, Latin or Arabic. His

last missionary journey was to Algiers where he was stoned to death.

Lost Property: If you have lost something, tell the hall porter or a person in charge wherever you are staying. Lost property offices are usually at the local *ayuntamiento* (town hall). In Palma, it's on Pl Cort. If the loss is serious, report it to the local police and get a copy of your statement. Promptly advise credit card companies, issuers of traveller's cheques and, if your passport is lost, your consulate.

Magalluf: See **Palma Nova** and **Magalluf**.

Mail: *Correos*, post offices, are open for general business Mon.-Fri. 0900-1300 and 1600-1900 Sat. half day. In some resorts they may be in caravans and only open during the main season. In Palma, the main post office is on Pl Constitucio. You can have your mail addressed here: Name, Lista de Correos, Pl Constitució, Palma de Majorca, Spain. Take your passport as identifiction when collecting. Stamps (*sellos*) can also be bought from hotels or tobacconists (*estancos* or *tabocos*). Mail boxes are yellow and red. Slots marked *extranjero* are for mail going beyond Spain.

Media: *El Día 16* and *Diario de Mallorca* are locally published daily newspapers in the Castilian language. The Barcelona edition of *El Pais*, Spain's newspaper with the highest international reputation, is available. *Cambio 16* is the top weekly news magazine. The English-language *Mallorca Daily Bulletin* gives some coverage of international, Spanish and island news. Leading foreign newspapers and magazines are widely available, many on their day of publication. Around 20 radio stations are available on AM and FM. Try 103.2FM for English Broadcasts, 88.8FM for German. Overseas services of some other countries can be picked up on medium or short wave.
The national television company TVE presents two channels in Castilian. Between 1230 and 1300 from June to September, Channel 2 features news in French, English and German. TV3 is a Catalan channel. Increasingly, hotel, apartment and villa complexes are offering cable and satellite channels.

Medical Treatment: It is foolhardy to travel without having a valid Travel Insurance Policy which provides substantial Accident and Health cover. Take a copy of the policy with you and make a separate note of its details and any emergency telephone numbers. On Majorca, your hotel will assist in calling a doctor or making an appointment with doctors or dentists. Your consulate may provide lists of medical practitioners. You will be required to pay for each visit or consultation. Emergency cases are usually accepted at both public and private clinics or hospitals. Unless you have obtained a card enabling you to Spanish public health services, you will be charged for these services in the same way as by private clinics. On presentation of your insurance policy, practitioners and clinics may accept waiting for payment of large bills form the insurers.

Farmacias (green cross sign) are chemist shops where prescriptions are obtained. A notice on the door will give the address of the nearest on duty chemist after normal hours. Prescription medicines are relatively inexpensive. Obtain and keep all receipts for subsequent submission to your insurers.

Miró, Joan: Born Barcelona 1893; moved to Majorca 1940; died there 1983. While living in Paris during the 1920s he gained international recognition as a leading surrealist. As a painter, designer, sculptor and ceramicist, his use of colour, form, space and symbolism was superb. He retained his position as one of the world's foremost artists until his death.

Monasteries: Accommodation is available in some of the island's monasteries and sanctuaries. It is inexpensive and ranges from the *hostal*-like facilities to be found at Lluc to the spartan cells at San Salvador (see **BUILDINGS**). Others to try (no advance bookings) include: Cura, Santuario La Victoria (Pollensa), Ermita Puig de Maria (Pollensa), Ermita Santa Magdalena (Inca), Santuario de Montesión (Porreras).

Money: The peseta (ptas.) is Spain's monetary unit. Notes: 10,000, 5,000, 2,000, 1,000 and 500, 200, 100 (going out of circulation). Coins: 500, 200, 100, 50, 25, 10, 5, 1. Banks offer the best exchange

Calas de Majorca

rate. Essential to present your passport for any transaction. The major international credit and charge cards are widely accepted, as are traveller's cheques in any west European currency or US dollars and Eurocheques supported by a valid card.

Moors: The collective word describing Arab, Berber and other Moslems who invaded from North Africa in 711 and rapidly gained control of the peninsula. They raided Majorca continuously until it was incorporated into their domain in 902. Christians who paid their taxes went unmolested and the island benefited from the advanced culture and techniques of irrigation and agriculture the Moors brought. Following the collapse of the Caliphate of Cordoba early in the 11thC, Majorca come under the rule of *walis*, minor kings who treated the islanders harshly. They were replaced by a new wave of North Africans, the Almoravides, who allowed the remaining Christians to follow their religion and advanced the island's agriculture and trade. Persecution started again and progress was halted with the arrival in 1203 of the Almohades. But their stay was short for on December 31, 1229 King Jaime and his Catalan army breached the walls of Medina Mayurka (Palma) and captured its ruler, Abu Yahya.

Motoring: You need the following with you when driving: passport, current driving licence (international or EC), vehicle registration document, third-party insurance document and bail bond (usually covered by car-hire agreement document), spare headlight, sidelight and rearlight bulbs, red warning triangle (if you're going on motorways). Minimum age is 18. Drive on the right. Overtake on the left. Give way to traffic coming from the right, especially at roundabouts, unless it is clearly marked that your road has priority. Never cross a solid white line to overtake or turn left. Always use indicators before overtaking or turning. Speed limits are: 60 kph most urban roads; 90 kph other roads where indicated; 100 kph main roads; 120 kph motorways. Belts must be worn in front seats outside urban areas. No hooting in urban areas unless in an emergency. Lights must be dipped for oncoming traffic. Don't drink and drive (permitted maximum is 0.8g alcohol per 1000cc). Penalties for offences can be severe and include prison terms.

Parking prohibitions are usually clearly marked by painted kerbstones and signs. A leaflet available from car-hire firms and tourist offices explains Palma's restricted parking system known as ORA. Some petrol stations close on Sundays and holidays. If your car breaks down or is involved in an accident, contact the car-hire firm for instructions.

Mountains: The chain rising steeply above the western and north-western coastline, from Andraitx to Formentor, creates the island's most spectacular scenery of barren crags, pine-covered slopes and verdant valleys. It hides small villages, tiny coves, fishing hamlets and stone-built terraces where olive, almond and citrus trees grow. Within a short distance the scene can change from barren and dramatic to quaint and picturesque. Often covered in mist, Puig Mayor rises to 1443 m; south across the Soller valley is Puig Teix (1062 m); looming above Estellencs and Galilea there's Puig Galatza (1026 m). On the southern edge of the central plain, Puig Randa stands proudly at 542 m. The Serranía de Levante is a low line of hills running along the east coast.

Music: See MUSIC, DANCE AND DRAMA, NIGHTLIFE, Flamenco, Folklore.

Other events include: Flamenco Festival, end April; Jazz Festival, July/August; Chopin International Piano Competition, November. Check with the Tourist Office.

Nudism: Women go topless on any beach and poolside. Both sexes strip totally on Playa Mago and Playa Es Trenc and in some secluded coves. A few hotels have terraces set aside for nude sunbathing. See BEACHES.

Paguera: It has a good range of hotels and apartments, some with exceptional locations, and budget eating places. Scandinavians and Germans outnumber the British here. The resort is well located for hiking, cycling and riding excursions through pretty countryside. See RESORTS 1 and 2. See also **Cala Mayor**.

Palma: The capital city is a stylish, all-year-round destination which offers the island's best choice of sophisticated hotels, restaurants, shopping and entertainment. Also the most places of historic and cultural interest. Palma is the best centre from which to make excursions by public transport to the rest of the island. See TOPICS.

Palma Nova and Magalluf: Against a backdrop of pine-covered hills, hotel, apartment and commercial blocks follow the curves of two wide bays and their golden sandy beaches. Most are geared to giving North Europeans a lot of hectic action and value for money by day and night. Magalluf has the island's only casino as well as a good choice of sports and attractions for kids. Portals Vells and Cala Figuera are just two of the pretty wooded coves to the south best reached by boat. The OIT office is in Roulotte on Av de Magaluf. See RESORTS 1.

Passports, Visas: Tourists holding a valid passport of a European Community country or of the United States and Canada do not require a visa to enter Spain. Those with Australian, New Zealand, South African, Japanese and some other passports, have to obtain a visa from a Spanish Consulate. Check with travel agent, tour operator or Spanish consulate.

Petra: See TOWNS & VILLAGES 2; Serra, Junipero.

Pets: Get details about importation of pets from a Spanish consulate in your country and also check regulations about bringing the pets back home. Not many hotels, apartments or villas on Majorca welcome pets.

Photography: The island is very photogenic. Make allowances for bright sunlight and glare. Because of midday haze, early morning and late afternoon are the best times for panoramic shots. Keep film and cameras out of heat and away from sand and sea. Do not attempt to photograph policemen or military personnel and installations. Photography, or use of flashlight, is not allowed in some tourist attractions. Film, development and printing is generally higher-priced in Spain than in other European countries. Rapid processing places give the standard quality service.

Pla, Es: 'The Plain' occupies the centre of the island where a quiet pace of life on small farms, in dusty villages and market towns is largely undisturbed by the foreign invasion of the coastline. A huge well lies below, from which windmills and pumps draw water to feed the patchwork of fields and orchards producing crops of almonds, figs, cherries, pears, citrus fruits, vegetables, salads, as well as animal feeds. Around Binissalem and Felanitx, vineyards predominate. Pig-rearing is the main livestock trade. Manacor and Inca have light industries derived from traditional crafts whose products have a market among tourists.

Playa de Canyamel: See Cala Millor.

Playas de Majorca: See Puerto de Alcudia.

Playas de Muro: See Ca'n Picafort.

Playas de Palma: Includes Cala Gamba, Ca'n Pastilla, El Arenal, Cala Blava. These resorts cater mostly for British and German package tourists and in high summer are noisy and congested. Ca'n Pastilla's proximity to the airport adds to the noise levels there. Son Veri and

Cala Blava are the quieter parts. Good sports amenities are plentiful. *Balnearios* (refreshment and service areas) and children's play areas are spaced along the beach which gets very crowded at Ca'n Pastilla and El Arenal. There are small coves at either end of the playa. The OIT office is at Marbella, telephone 26 76 54. See **RESORTS 1**

Police: The *Policía Nacional* are the tough, smart-looking men and women in khaki and brown uniforms and berets who walk the streets in twos and patrol in white or tan vehicles. Report any crime to them and make a formal statement at their comisaría. Their headquarters is at c/ Ruiz de Alda 1, Palma, Tel 28 04 00. *Policía Municipal* (blue uniforms, white or blue cars) deal mainly with urban traffic and enforcing munici- pal regulations. In some resorts they may be assisted by corps of *Policía Turística* in high season. You'll see the *Guardia Civil* (green uniforms and tricorn hats or soft caps) at immigration and customs posts and patrolling roads, the coastline and rural areas.

Portals Nous: See **RESORTS 1** .

Porto Colom: See **RESORTS 3**.

Porto Cristo: The nearby caves of Drach and Ham are the principal attraction for day trippers to this small port. Bigger tourist development is northwards at S'Illot, Cala Moreya and Sa Coma which have better, sandy beaches and are still popular with local people from nearby vil- lages. To the south, Porto Cristo Novo and Cala Estany have secluded sandy coves. OIT office - Gual. See **RESORTS 3**.

Porto Cristo Novo: See Porto Cristo.

Porto Petro: See Cala d'Or.

Prehistory: The poblado of Capicorp Vell, south of Llucmayor, is the island's best-preserved Bronze Age settlement. There are excavated houses, tunnels and two talayots. Ask at the house opposite to gain entry. Near Arta are Ses Paisses, lesser remains of another settlement, and the talayots of Sa Canova. Near Son Baul, remains of the 7thC BC Necròpolis de Son Real.

Public Holidays: Public Holidays are celebrated on Majorca on the following days: 1 Jan, 6 Jan, 19 Mar, 1 May, 24 Jun, 29 Jun, 25 Jul, 28 Jul, 15 Aug, 12 Oct, 1 Nov, 8 Dec, 25 Dec, 31 Dec and on the variable feast days of Good Friday, Easter Monday and Corpus Christi. Additionally, towns and villages have their particular fiesta days which are also public holidays.

Public Toilets: Few and far between. Choose a bar or cafe, use its facilities, then, though it's not obligatory, have something to drink there.

Puerto de Alcudia: Young crowds give the resort a lively pace in high season. The area has comprehensive leisure, sports and entertainment facilities. The old town of Alcudia is interesting for some sightseeing and shopping and, as from Puerto de Pollensa and Ca'n Picafort,

Porto Cristo

there's a good choice of excursions, which includes exploring small canals by water scooter. The Playas de Majorca are a long stretch of beach with fine white sand. The OIT office is on Edificio Xara. See **RESORTS 2**.

Puerto de Andraitx: A small fishing village with a now burgeoning tourist industry. It is a good centre for walking or sight-seeing by car or boat. A good beach, with some amenities, is at Camp de Mar which also has the higher-rated hotels and is a popular stop for excursion boats. Another good beach is at San Telmo; also simple accommodation and eating places. San Telmo faces the bird sanctuary of Dragonera island, another excursion destination.
See **RESORTS 2**.

Puerto de Pollensa: The areas around the port, including Cala San Vicente and Formentor, are popular with a wide range and mix of ages and nationalities. Early and late season, and in winter, it's a favourite of the older generation. Rides and walks in the surrounding countryside are rewarded with lovely views and there's a variety of organized trips by boat. Along the horseshoe Bahía Pollensa, the beaches are long and open or smaller and pine-shaded. At Cala San Vicente, which has grown rapidly as a resort, there's a choice of three beaches (sandy, rocky or pebbly). Playa Formentor's long sandy stretch is bordered by pines and there are more intimate coves along the cabo. The area's nightlife centres on bars, restaurants, a few discos and entertainments put on by the hotels. Pollensa town has a few sights and worthwhile arts and crafts shops. The OIT office is to be found on Miquel Capllonch. See **RESORTS 2**.

Puerto de Soller: Day trippers from Palma and other resorts crowd both the town of Soller and Puerto de Soller. This picturesque port has always been popular with French families. It is a good base for excursions by horse taxi, car or on foot into lovely countryside and dramatic mountain areas. Calobra, Truent and many other pretty coves with tiny beaches can be visited by boat. The OIT office is located on Cañónigo Oliver, telephone 63 01 01. See **EXCURSIONS - COACH & TRAIN, RESORTS 2**.

Porto Soller

Religious Services: Services in English: *Anglican*: Nunez de Balboa 6, Son Armadans, Palma, 0830 and 1100 Sun, 1030 Wed. *Catholic:* San Augustin, Pl Santa Monica, Palma, 1000 Sun; San Fernando, Ctra Arenal 308, Sal Maravillas, 1130 Sun; San Lorenzo, Palma Nova, 1000 Sun; Santa Brigida, Miguel Rossello Alemany 18, Cala Mayor, 1000 Sun. *Baptist Mission,* Aragon 34 Apt 4b, 2030 Wed. *Full Gospel Fellowship,* Juan Alcover 13, Palma Nova, 1000 Sun. *Salvation Army*, Hotel Barbados Sol, Palma Nova, 1100 Sun, 2030 Wed. *Ecumenical Mass,* Palma Cathedral 1000 Sun; *Jewish Service*, Monsenor Palmer 3, 1800 Fri; *Zen Centre*, San Felio 8; *Baha'i Centre* Gabriel Llabres 25; *Mormon Church*, Marques le la Cenia, 1200 Sun; *Seventh Day Adventist,* Despuig 22; *Reformed Baptist,* Ortega ya Gasset 15.

Restaurants: See RESTAURANTS, **Eating Places, Food.**

Sa Coma: See **Porto Cristo**.

Sailing, Watersports: With 30 *clubs náuticos* and their 10,000

berths, plus many more private marinas, Majorca is a proven favourite of the yachting fraternity. Specialist holiday operators offer sailing 'packages' and yachts can be chartered locally. Your regular yachting magazine is likely to have advertisements. Lessons in dinghy sailing, waterskiing and windsurfing are available in marinas and on many beaches; there's no shortage of places hiring boats and gear, also pedalos and open canoes.

Salvador, Ludwig: An Austrian archduke, visited Majorca in 1867, loved it, returned to settle permanently, bought large estates on the west coast and became an enthusiastic publicist of the island's charms. He entertained famous and influential people at his homes of Son Marroig and Miramar, introducing them to Majorca, and produced a nine-volume appreciation of the island and its people, Die Balearen in Wort und Bild.

San Agustín: See **Cala Mayor**.

San Telmo: See **Puerto de Andraitx**.

Santa Ponsa: Similar to Palma Nova and Magalluf but a slightly quieter pace. It has up-market parts near the smart marina and is set to become the island's golfing centre. The gently sloping beach with good sand is well served with amenities. The OIT office is to be found on Ramón de Moncada. See **RESORTS 1**.

Serra, Junipero: The Franciscan friar, who was born of farming folk in Petra and left for the New World in 1749. He helped to set up many of the mission stations (named after the statues of saints in his hometown's San Bernadino church) which later grew into the towns and cities of California.

Shopping: See **SHOPPING, Best Buys, Hours and Hypermarkets**.

S'Illot: See **Porto Cristo**.

Son Vida: See **RESORTS 1 - Palma**.

Sports: See **Fishing, Golf, Horseriding, Sailing and Watersports, Tennis.** Many more sports can be practised on the island: Scuba-diving, flying, hang-gliding, parachute-jumping, billiards, bowling, squash, table tennis. You can go and watch football, basketball and *pelota* matches; cycle, horse-trotting and dog races. Details from local tourist offices and newspapers.

Talayots: Stone towers built from about 1300 to 100 BC in settlements like Capicorp Vell or in high, isolated positions, where they may have been watchtowers. Remains of several hundred are scattered around the island. See **Prehistory**.

Tapas: Many bars serve these tempting appetizers, ranging from olives, nuts or crisps to small and tasty portions of meats, seafoods,

omelettes, salads or vegetables. Some are served hot. *Raciones* are larger portions of the same things.

Taxis: Inexpensive by international comparison. They're free when
showing a libre sign on the windscreen and a small green light on the
roof. A list of supplements which may be added to the metered fare is
shown in the cab. Taxis without meters charge officially fixed fares.
Fares are higher after 2100 and at weekends. It's always wise to get an
idea of what your journey is going to cost.

Telephone, Telex, Fax: Hotels tend to add a big margin to the cost
of communications services. *Telephone*: Area code is 971. Cheap rate
is from 2200-0800. Coin-operated booths require 5, 25 or 100 ptas
coins. Place coins in sloping groove at top of coin box. Lift receiver,
check for dial tone, then dial. Coins will drop into box as needed.
Codes for Spanish provinces and other countries are given in the
booths. For local calls dial the number only. For international calls,
after dial tone, dial 07, wait for second dial tone, then dial country
code plus area code (exclude initial 0) plus number. At the Telefonica
offices in Palma (Av Rey Jaime III 20 and c/ Constitucio 1) and cabins,
which are operated in many resorts during the season, payment is easi-
er (after the call) and assistance is available. *Telex and Fax* at main post
office and from business services bureaux. *Telegram*: by telephone on
722 20 00 and at Post Offices.

Tennis: Take your racket. With some 25 tennis clubs and many courts
at hotels, apartments, vacation villages, golf and other sports clubs,
there are plenty of places to play. Many courts have floodlights.

Time Differences: Same time zone as mainland Spain and the rest
of Western Europe: one hour ahead of GMT and 6-12 hours later than
the USA.

Tipping: Although it may not be shown separately, a service charge is
included on all hotel and restaurant bills. But it's still the practice to
leave around 5 to 10% in restaurants and to tip hotel staff for special

services. At the bar, leave a token tip; leave 5 to 10% for table service. Taxi drivers, hairdressers and tour guides usually get around 10%. Lavatory attendants, doormen, shoeshines and car-parking attendants - 25-100 ptas.

Tourism: Mass tourism to Majorca began in the late fifties and has transformed an economically backward region into a honey pot for Spanish and international property developers and holiday operators. Younger members of subsistence farming and fishing families were drawn to earn wages in the new resorts and immigrants came from other poor parts of Spain. Now, about 60% of the island's income is contributed by tourism. Much of its infrastructure is controlled by foreigners, including some of the bigger European holiday operators. Nearly 5.5 million visitors annually pass through its airport (one of the busiest in Europe during the summer) or arrive by sea. The British make up the largest contingent with around 1.8 million visits, followed by West Germans (1.3), Spanish nationals (0.52), Scandinavians (0.45), French (0.25), Benelux nationals (0.24). The majority go for sun, sea and simple pleasure on low-cost 'packages'. Many are faithful regulars. There's also an up-market tourism element centred on luxury residential estates, marinas (where expensive yachts glisten in the sun) and converted inland properties.

Tourist Information: Spanish National Tourist Offices in: Brussels, Buenos Aires, Copenhagen, Chicago, Dusseldorf, Frankfurt, Geneva, Helsinki, Houston, The Hague, Lisbon, London, Los Angeles, Mexico City, Milan, Munich, New York, Oslo, Paris, Rome, San Augustin, Stockholm, Sydney, Tokyo, Toronto, Vienna, Zurich. Central Tourist Office of the Gobern Balear (Regional Government) is at Av Rey Jaime III 10, Palma (Tel 71 22 16) and of Palma Municipality at Santo Domingo 11 (Tel 72 40 90).
Tourist Offices cannot make reservations.

Villas and Apartments: A few holiday operators specialize in this type of accommodation which can vary from studios amidst the concrete jungle of a busy resort to a luxuriously converted finca (farmhouse) in an idyllic rural setting.
Agencies and individuals advertise in the holiday sections of quality newspapers in Britain, West Germany and some other countries.
Agencias de alquiler on the island also offer properties to let, mostly for a minimum period of one month.

Walk: For many of its regular visitors, the number of delightful walks which can be taken on the island are top among its attractions. They vary from short, gentle strolls to arduous whole-day treks. Local tourist offices will supply information. Never walk alone, don't be too ambitious, wear sensible shoes and a hat, carry an item of warmer clothing, water and a snack.

What's On: Look for leaflets and posters at your hotel, tourist offices and travel agents. Billboards advertise events. See **Media** for local newspapers which have listings.

Windmills: The smaller of the two types of *molinos* are those which pump water from the plentiful subterranean supply with which the island is blessed. More solidly built, of stone, and comprising three floors are the old grain mills, some of which have now been converted into homes.

Wines: *Vino*, or *vi* in Catalan is *tinto* red; *blanco* white or *rosaso* rosé. Island reds from Binissalem are dark and heavy, often rough. Binissalem and Felanitx produce a small amount of white wine, quite light and palatable. For quality wines choose one from Spain's *denominaciones de origen*, officially demarcated and controlled wine growing areas, like Rioja and Penedes which have achieved the highest reputation internationally. Many restaurants will have a *vino de la casa*, house wine. Regional restaurants will feature wines from their region of Spain. See what other diners, preferably local people, have ordered. Ask the waiter for advice if you are unsure.